THE STORY OF
SCOTTISH
COUNTRY DANCING

THE DARLING DIVERSION
EVELYN M. HOOD

COLLINS

For Angus

The cover illustration is *Reeling* from an original watercolour
drawing by Charles Williams, c. 1815, in the
John Telfer Dunbar collection. Reproduced by permission.
The tartan is MacDonald.

First published 1980
Published by William Collins Sons and Company Limited
© 1980 Evelyn M. Hood
ISBN 0 00 411110 9
Printed in Great Britain

CONTENTS

ACKNOWLEDGEMENTS

My most grateful thanks are due to a host of people who have helped me prepare this book.

To begin with there are those dozens of people who wrote to me from all over the world with their memories of their Scottish dancing days, when, some years ago, I was preparing the scripts for Grampian Television's programme series *The Scottish Dance*. The response I received then to a request for information motivated the writing of this book since, it seemed to me, the writers evinced a tremendous interest in the subject of the history of dancing in Scotland.

My particular thanks are due to the late Dr Jean Milligan who, for the TV series and for this book, was my guide, mentor, enthusiastic encourager and, best of all, friend.

I sought help from, and was generously assisted by the staffs of the following libraries: the Reference Departments of Dundee and Aberdeen Public Libraries; the Edinburgh Room and the Music Department of Edinburgh Central Library; the National Library of Scotland; the Vaughan Williams Library at Cecil Sharp House, London; the Sandeman Library, Perth and Blairgowrie Public Library.

I was greatly assisted by the staff of the Bibliothèque Nationale de France in Paris and by Raymond Vaillant, assistant librarian of the Museum and Library of the Paris Opéra who so patiently guided me through the International Dance Archives, housed at the Opéra. Assistance was also given me in France by M. Chaumoin of *Le Chardon d'Ecosse* Club and Madame Laurèce Geddes of the Musée Carnavalet, Paris.

Mrs Isobel Cramb of Aberdeen has been most generous to me with help and advice for which I am very grateful. My thanks are due, too, to Mr Bobby Watson, Aberdeen; to Mr and Mrs Neill Macfarlane of Forfar; to Mr George Peterson, Brae, Shetland; the curators of the Black Watch and the Argyll and Sutherland Highlanders Regimental Museums; to the Royal Scottish Country Dance Society and the Society's headquarters' staff in Edinburgh; to Mrs E. Young for undertaking to type the manuscript; and to Angus, Jonathan, Gillian and Peter Hood for their encouragement and tolerance in the past months.

INTRODUCTION

As if to underline the truth of real tradition, most Scots take
their native dancing absolutely for granted. If they are over
twenty-one, they will at least have learned the Petronella or a
Dashing White Sergeant at school. It would be a poor Hogmanay
without an Eightsome or a Strip the Willow. And the end of a
perfect evening among friends often involves the dance ritual
of standing up, joining hands in a ring and singing Auld Lang
Syne – even although few get the wordy bits quite right!

Even in the centre of Lowland Fife a 'Highland' Gathering
would be unthinkable without its proper quota of skilled
dancers competing with each other in elegant footwork, and
tiny, bobbing, kilted ducklings making heavy-footed sense of a
Highland Fling. Dancing is as much a part of Scotland as lochs,
bens, glens and pure malt.

There are those who care enough about our native dancing to
become members of the Royal Scottish Country Dance Society,
learning the delights of the most beautiful formation dancing.
And there are those of even greater aspirations, who are trained
from childhood to the intricacies of the step dances which are
basically balletic in form and execution.

There are others – the remaining five million or so – who
simply dance as the mood takes them and they can fling
themselves into a dance in a way that belies any south-of-the-
Border notion of the inhibited, dour Scot. In Scotland we
possess a treasure trove of national dances and national music.
Although, immediately, we encounter the vexed question of
what *is* the 'Scottish' nation.

Centuries of troubled history have divided the country into
two almost distinct cultural groups. 'Almost' because, of course,
in cultural matters there are always grey areas which defy neat
separation into black and white.

Original inhabitants have left no traces, and Scots today must
dig for their roots in a tangle of flintmakers who came here from
all the airts, Beaker Folk, builders of chambered cairns, and the
men of the Iron Age – the broch builders, some of whose
sheltering towers still stand like sentinels keeping watch along
the eastern seaboard.

Around 500 BC the Celtic line entered the tangle – a great wave of people who eventually dominated the whole country and remained in command for over a thousand years. Proud and industrious, the Celtic tribes cultivated as well as conquered. In due course they had to deal, quite successfully, with repeated incursions by the Romans who called the land they raided Caledonia.

When the Romans encountered the Celts they dubbed them Picts because of their habit of ceremonially painting themselves. But the Celts were hardly the crude savages found in Victorian depictions of the glories of the Roman Occupation. A better portrait can perhaps be painted in the mind's eye after looking at their clasps, buckles and other ornaments displayed in Scotland's numerous museums.

For the Romans discretion proved the better part of valour. Despite an overwhelming victory at Mons Graupius around AD 84, they had found it inexpedient, if not impossible, to plant a Roman root to thrive in such a place, and they left to shelter behind Hadrian's Wall.

Even at this very dim point in Scotland's past, there is evidence of divisions between the tribes. The people who had settled to the east and south of the Grampian Mountains already considered themselves to be a distinct group from the Caledonii of the west and north.

In the centuries which followed, a series of invasions all left their mark – Scots, Vikings, Danes, Jutes, and eventually the Normans all affected Scotland. But throughout the invasions the country never lost but rather had reinforced that cultural and tribal division between the mountainous Highland west and north and the Lowland north-east, east and south.

A division which gives us stories of wild sword dances, remnants of mime dances, footfalls from centuries back, which endure in Highland places, and the haunting nine-note music of the bagpipes. A division which makes the fiddle the traditional accompaniment to dancing in the east and which makes the dancing itself of a different sort – a marriage of courtly and country modes.

A division which in the story of dancing in Scotland liberally sprinkles traps for the historian who chooses to ignore references to a *piper* playing for 'Maggie Lauder' at Ainster Fair in Fife on the east coast; or for one who would fail to acknowledge that much of what is now known as Highland dancing is the result of the work of *Lowland* dancing masters of the 18th, 19th and 20th centuries. As the story of social dancing in Scotland unfolds, it is hoped then that 'grey areas' will be taken for what they are.

When today's Scot responds to the call: 'Take partners for an

Eightsome Reel!', he is most likely to dance unaware that he is performing a 19th-century dance with movements culled from preceding centuries. In the Eightsome Reel is found the ring dance, the chain, circling round an object or person to be venerated, the setting and turning of the most ancient of reels and the movement of the ring clockwise and anti-clockwise. Much he cares as he throws up his arms, leaps wildly and boldly in the centre of the ring, striking attitudes of ballet, if he but knew it. And to cap it all, something prompts him to cry out 'hooch' (the 'ch' as in loch) with each new upsweeping phrase of music.

Purists may not admire his style, but must wonder how he can tell, by what instinct does he know, the phrasing of the dance. And what prompts him to hop as he moves and not 'walk' through the figures of the dance as is the manner of the English or North American country dances?

Any attempt to answer such questions would generate a deal more heat than light on the subject of social dancing in Lowland Scotland. Suffice it to say that the Scots do dance and when they dance they enjoy social dancing which has a long and interesting history likely to have begun with time itself. As one French writer on dancing put it in the 17th century, 'since there has been man, there has been dancing'.

All over the world there are folk dance societies, groups which exist to discover and revive dances long since passed out of common usage.

In the Eastern European states, large sums of money are spent in subsidizing 'State' folk dance and music groups. These are teams of professional dancers and musicians paid to maintain something which cannot in all honesty be called folk if by 'folk' one means 'of the people'.

In Western Europe in recent years there has been a great revival of interest in the old songs and dances. France now has dozens of 'folklorique' groups happily ferreting through music libraries and old dance manuals and reviving 'folk' dances long since lapsed. On fêtes and fairdays these dances are brought out for demonstration to entertain spectators – rarely are they a matter of general participation. Perhaps the day will come when such revived social dances will lose their special exhibit quality and become truly the dances of the people once more. This keep-it-in-a-glass-case-and-bring-it-out-on-Sundays kind of 'folk' dancing has no bearing whatever on the Scottish social dance.

There *are* Scottish dances which have gone into the 'museum' and are taken out for display from time to time. For example, in recent years, a group in the Lothians has successfully revived a Morris dancing group, which the majority of Scots erroneously assume to have been an exclusively English activity.

But the mainstream of Lowland Scottish dancing is social dancing which developed over the centuries into the kind of dance suitable for performing in the ballroom. It is this ballroom social dancing which attracts hundreds of thousands of people – frequently of non-Scottish origin – to take up Scottish country dancing.

There are branches of the Royal Scottish Country Dance Society all over the world dedicated to the teaching and enjoyment of Scottish dancing. Throughout the former Empire and Colonies, Scottish dancing clubs abound. Wherever the Scots colonized in number, their descendants turn out to dance regularly in their thousands.

Canada boasts over 2700 branches of the Society and there is an affiliated group which dances regularly in Port Moresby, New Guinea, in temperatures which overwhelm both mad dogs *and* Englishmen! New Zealand has over a thousand branches and there are hundreds of other clubs linked to Caledonian societies.

These clubs exist for sound historical and ethnological reasons. Less easily explained is the fascination that Scottish dancing holds for those who have no special ties with Scotland. There are seventy-five branches of the R.S.C.D.S. in Holland, alone, sixty-three in Sweden and the Japanese have taken to Scottish country dancing as passionately as they took to whisky and golf.

This book is not intended to be an erudite study of dance history. It is simply an attempt to tell some of the story of dancing in Lowland Scotland. Serious students should hasten to the superb books on the subject by George S. Emerson or J. F. and T. M. Flett. If, indeed, this book sends readers in search of further information, then the author will be extremely happy.

Dancers will find no instruction here on how to dance better. It is hoped, however, that anyone who has ever wondered why, in Scotland, we dance the dances we dance, may find some of the answers in this book.

1

TRACES AND ORIGINS

'Dancing,' a learned professor declared in the 1930s, 'is the ordered and more or less rhythmic expression of an impulse of movement . . . it only occurs in an abnormal condition; no animal or primitive human being dances unless urged to by some specific excitement.'

Yet there is not a nation in the world without some sort of dance tradition. Since primitive times, man has frequently felt the urge to show that 'more or less rhythmic expression of an impulse of movement'. What distinguishes one nation from another is the manner and form of that expression. And what distinguishes primitive man from later man is that the latter learned there was pleasure to be had from the function of dancing without having to be urged to do it 'by some specific excitement'.

Primitive man at the mercy of the seasons, in constant battle with the elements, unsure about his interpretations of yesterday and tormented by doubts about tomorrow, danced for many reasons. He still does – in the rain forests of Africa and South America.

Primitive Western man obeyed the same urges and suffered the same fears. He danced to placate the gods. He danced to cure illness and bring rain. He danced to ask for the rains to stop. He danced to show his prowess as a hunter and as a fighter. As he danced for rain he might have imitated the falling of raindrops with a light tapping of his feet. A dance before a hunt would probably have shown some parody of the animal to be hunted or the fish to be caught. In ritual dances performed to placate gods or to worship a divine relic, the dance would take the form of a ritual ring weaving round the object of veneration in the centre.

Because the gods were believed to order the seasons and direct the movement of sun, moon and stars, it was natural that men would attempt to imitate the divine patterns in ritual dancing – to travel in circles according to the movement of the sun, particularly since the sun was the giver of good; clockwise, we call it, to the left. Travelling to the right – against the sun, and consequently against good spirits, was to turn 'widdershins'.

The earliest Christian missionaries had few scruples about

adopting pagan rituals and adapting them to their own uses and ends. If the people of an area were in the habit of celebrating a certain ritual at a certain time – a fire festival to worship the sun or encourage its return after a dark long winter, then who were the churchmen to pass up a chance of hitching that ritual to some Christian commemoration. If a dance or two placated and pleased the gods of the harvest, they might equally delight the God of love.

This was sound reasoning, with scriptural backing. If King David, the psalmist, could sing, 'Thou hast turned for me my mourning into dancing', then surely so could any other mortal who had been afflicted like David. It was this kind of argument which Scotland's Church Reformers of much later date found so hard to refute when they wanted to ban social dancing!

In every part of Scotland where Roman Christianity took root – and in those parts where it was hardly known at all, where folk adhered to the old Irish-Celtic ways because no one had yet come to tell them any different – dance rituals continued despite new management.

Throughout Scotland to this day it is possible to find traditions which are evident happy blends of pagan and Christian. In Lanark the annual children's festival of Whuppity Stourie is one such tradition. This takes place in the town of Lanark each year on the first of March. Marian McNeill in Volume Four of *The Silver Bough* describes the ceremony thus . . .

'From the month of October to the month of February inclusive, the bells in the Parish Church cease to ring at six in the evening, but resume at the same hour on the first day of March. The children of the town gather in great numbers at the Cross, where the Parish Church stands, and at the first sound of the bells they set off, shouting and jostling, each whirling round his head a closely rolled ball of paper attached to a string about two feet long, and rush around the church beating one another with their swinging balls of paper, until the bells have stopped pealing.'

Different theories are propounded as to the origins of this ceremony but Miss McNeill offered her own explanation '. . . it arose as an exorcism of evil spirits. (Compare the swinging of fireballs on Hogmanay at Stonehaven.) Our forefathers believed that these evil spirits travelled in clouds of dust (stour) and were given to casting a blight on crops in springtime. They had to be exorcised, and that exorcism was attained, as in many European countries, by clashing metals together. In Scotland this is achieved by ringing church bells, beating trays and so forth on Hogmanay, a rite originally meant to drive out all the evil influences that might have accumulated in home or burgh throughout the year.'

It may have been galling to early Christian church builders in this country to find themselves accepted by dint of the loudness of their bells. The louder they were, the more efficacious in ridding the countryside of evil spirits!

Added insurance against malignant spirits came in the form of May Games or May Festivals involving rites which mingled dew – the Druids' holy water – with hilltop Christian services and dancing round the maypole or doing honour to a May Queen. May rituals were almost entirely fertility rituals. Many girls in Scotland still go out to wash their faces in the May dew and make a wish. And May Queens are still chosen for crowning at village galas and festivals. The significance of choosing a young nubile lass as a symbol of fertility is the last thing in the minds of today's organizing committees, but the choice of a girl as a focus of veneration at May time has been going on in this land for countless centuries. Maypole dances with their clockwise and widdershins weavings and twinings also had a ritual significance, but sadly they are no longer ritually performed in Scotland and, indeed, have not been since the mid-17th century.

But for the ordinary man of earlier centuries the dreich calendar of a hard, and often hungry, year would be punctuated by glorious days of significant fun. 'Specific excitement' enough to make men – and women – dance.

With the marriage of King Malcolm Canmore, in 1070, to Margaret, an English princess, Scotland moved from comparative isolation into the European sphere of influence.

When Duke William of Normandy invaded England and King Harold was slain and the English defeated at Hastings in 1066, Edgar, Margaret's brother, thought it prudent to flee the country. He threw himself and his sister upon the mercy of the rough northern King Malcolm and was given shelter. Malcolm fell in love with Margaret and there was made a royal marriage which altered the path of Scotland's history.

For the first time in Scotland, the court included foreigners who had come with the fleeing English royal family – foreigners from as near as England and as far away as Hungary. They must have been appalled, as Margaret herself was, by the crude poverty of Scottish court life. Margaret, who was a woman of considerable willpower and determination, soon introduced elements of pure southern luxury to the old Celtic court.

It is not difficult to imagine that along with the beautifully decorated manuscripts and prayer books and the tapestries for covering bare walls that there would also have been imported music and instruments of a fine sort – and maybe Malcolm was the first Scottish king to have lessons in courtly dancing.

Malcolm and Margaret were succeeded by several of their sons, the youngest of whom, David I, can be said to have 'Normanized' Scotland. He married a Norman wife, adopted Norman ways, and when he came to rule his bleak northern homeland, in 1124, he brought with him Norman friends who were in their time to found some of Scotland's noblest families. These men rose with David against the more turbulent northern Celts who were in revolt against the incursion of Norman courtiers and traders, and clerics with new-fangled Roman rituals. By the end of the 12th century much of the country had been brought to the elegant, iron-armoured heel of feudalism.

In the end, only in the mountainous places did feudalism fail to conquer completely. The Celtic Mormaers or Earls – the ancient aristocracy – *did* pay lip-service to the system, whilst retaining their father-figure, robber-baron links with their people. (These links were still discernible six or seven hundred years later when the 18th- and 19th-century descendants of the Mormaers cleared the people from the glens, and those poor folk found that their only title to the land had been tradition.)

The feudalism that took hold in the east and south of Scotland was of a purer strain. Norman nobles, friends of successive kings, exiled and restored, were given lands and titles in exchange for favours shown. Burghs were founded by Royal Charter, whenever the king thought he stood to gain by the activities of the new merchant classes. How much this affected the ordinary daily life of the ordinary peasant Scotsman and woman is difficult to tell. As to the manner in which they took their pleasures, it is well nigh impossible to make anything except suppositions.

Feudalism and the establishment of the burghs might possibly have brought a greater feeling of security and order to the life of the Lowland Scot. But his worries about the vagaries of the seasons and having enough for himself and his family to eat would change little – no matter who sat in the castle or the manor house. He would have the same reasons to weep and to dance as he had always had.

The significant changes for him would have been the necessity to learn a little of My Lord's foreign tongue, taking some of the words for his own use, just as My Lord's name would in time become 'truly' Scottish – Sinclair, Melville, Bruce, Lindsay, Fraser, and the like.

It is from a Norman knight, Walter Espec, that we learn how the Scottish army advanced at the Battle of the Standard near Northallerton in 1138 in seeming undisciplined disarray.

'Before them go jugglers and dancers,' wrote Espec, 'before us the cross of Christ and the relics of the saints.'

'Jugglers' were the *jongleresca* – a word of Spanish origin signifying musicians – so we gather that 12th-century Scots went into battle with music and dancing.

'Who would not laugh rather than fear when the wretched bare-breeched Scots came up against such adversaries? What are these naked men to steel-clad Normans, their leather shields to our lances, their recklessness of death to our reasonable valour?'

To the knights of the south accustomed to other styles of dancing, the Scots' advance would indeed have made them seem like savages. But, if the musicians Espec saw that day were in fact 'jugglers', then the Scots could hardly have been the savages the English Normans supposed. Jugglers were, above all, itinerant musicians who went from castle to castle, entertaining wherever a nobleman and his men gathered. The presence of jugglers, therefore, indicates that such courtly entertainment had already found its place in the donjons and keeps of the new Scottish aristocracy.

Spring, summer and autumn days in Scotland must have held a particular charm for the feudal lords. The long hours that stretch fingers of light to span almost the twenty-four meant that any knight worth the salt above which he sat could be out in company of hawks and hounds in endless passionate pursuit of game and of the ideals of true chivalry.

The winter dark, on the other hand, seemed to last as long as the light of summer. Damp coursed down the stone walls, inside and out. The household – lords, ladies, squires, pages, and the multitude of hangers-on huddled round the main hall fire. On nights like these the jugglers, the balladeers, the singers and tellers of tales would be doubly welcome. There would be music, too, for dancing.

Sadly, the names of dances do not survive from these early times but the music provided for the dance and the dances themselves, thanks to the far-ranging jugglers, were probably a mixture of native and foreign imports. Although we must merely surmise the style of dancing, an illustration from a book of songs and the engraving on a 13th century brooch from Limoges offer us a tantalizing glimpse of the gracefulness of dancing in the age of chivalry.

By the end of the 13th century the Norman aristocracy had become so thoroughly established in Scotland as to be in contention for the throne. The ensuing struggle for the throne and against the hammering English invaders resulted in the emergence of a scion of Norman nobility as king, from 1306–29 – Robert the Bruce.

By the 14th century, Scotland's king and most of his lords had their own mummers – bands of players, jesters, singers and musicians who in the long summer days would double as stableboys, hawk-masters, fletchers, and the like. The mummers performed plays to celebrate a fête day or whenever guests were in residence.

Morris dancing, mummers' plays, May Day and May Queen celebrations are usually thought of as English activities. Certainly they have survived south of the Border in a purer, longer line of succession than north of it. But Scotland, too, had traditional mummers' plays, blackface dancers called Morrismen, Guisers and May Queens, Abbots of Misrule and Unreason, Robin Hood and all the other dramatis personae of this genre.

The performance of mummers' plays seems to have had two distinct venues, one being the great halls of the palaces and castles, the other the mercat cross of the burgh, on public feast days or holy days. The celebrations of these ancient feast days such as St James's fair in Cupar, Fife, and St Moluag's fair in Alyth, Perthshire, are now reduced to the appearance of a handful of sideshows and shooting galleries on common ground.

Burgh performances of the mummers' plays were fairly strictly controlled by the fathers of the councils – much as the modern Watch Committees kept a douce eye on X-certificate films! – and for much the same reasons. The safeguarding of public morality has been a long-standing preoccupation of our public figures. Scotland's early burgh records are liberally sprinkled with references to the appointing of official players in festival plays and of bringing them to book for misdeeds.

The two principal festivals in the year were May Day (Beltane), a celebration which marked the opening of a new growing season, and Hallowe'en, celebrated on the eve of All Saints' Day but so strongly associated with play acting and guising as to indicate an earlier pre-Christian celebration, possibly of the Harvest Home variety.

Guising has always been part of Hallowe'en. All over Scotland, to this very day, bands of young guisers go from door to door acting out a story, reciting a poem or rendering some choice item from the current pop charts in exchange for fruit, nuts or hard cash.

In the rural areas of eastern Scotland, Angus, Fife, the Lothians, the children spend time preparing their Hallowe'en guising performances and make masks or else blacken their faces. Around the Forfar area in the county of Angus, until very recent times, the children would go from door to door calling, 'Goloshens! Goloshens! It's the Goloshens!'

Goloshen? A corruption of Galatian who was a hero of Scottish mummers' plays performed at Hallowe'en, Beltane and

Old Yule. Goloshen was Scotland's equivalent of the English St George, and it has been suggested that his name was derived from Galgacus, leader of the Caledonians against the Romans.

Goloshen plays were in the same vein as most of the English mummers' plays. The hero had to overcome all sorts of adversaries and difficulties and the characters in the action included the Fool and the Doctor who endure as characters in English mummers' plays to this day. There is absolutely no certainty about the origins of play acting and guising at certain seasons of the year and we must be content with the fact that these plays are of great antiquity, and modern anthropologists believe that they have many connections with the ancient Celtic pre-Christian religions. In modern times it is regrettable that in some parts of Scotland, notably in Aberdeen, guising has become hopelessly confused with the celebration of Guy Fawkes' Night and in that city one is likely to be accosted by small guisers in blackface and fancy dress demanding simply: 'A penny for the Guy'.

In the matter of tradition, it is significant that, in the celebration of a festival such as Hallowe'en, remnants of ancient amusements can still be seen in rural Scotland. It is not so surprising, then, to discover in one of the remotest parts of all Scotland a truly remarkable relic of a mummers' play in the Morris tradition – the Sword Dance of Papa Stour – which combines ancient sword dancing with sword play and passing movements in one 'dance'. It is almost certain that this very old dance/play would have gone the way of all the others had it been the Sword Dance of Paisley or even of Peterhead.

But Papa Stour is a tiny island in the Shetlands – the most northerly group of the British Isles – and it lies off the westernmost tip of Mainland, the largest of the Shetland islands.

Papa Stour has a long and fascinating history, from Viking stronghold to leper colony. By the 1970s it had, in spite of North Sea oil discoveries around the islands, continued to depopulate in common with most of the smaller islands in the group.

When the Shetland islands came under the rule of Scotland as part of James III's wife's dowry, in 1469, bundles of islands and parcels of land were handed out to southern nobles who, when they travelled to investigate their new properties, undoubtedly brought with them their own retainers and entertainers to care for and amuse them in the manner to which they had been accustomed in the gentler more southerly mainland of Scotland.

Winter nights in Shetland are the longest in the country. Daylight shows only from nine a.m. to three p.m. in December and January and the great Viking festival of Up Helly-Aa at the end of January in the islands' capital, Lerwick, is a modern revival of an old celebration held to mark the stretching of the days.

The chief of the entire ceremony is the Guiser Jarl. Behind him follow teams of guisers. The burning of the great wooden longship marks the start of several days of revelry and entertainment. Dances are held in different parts of the town and, at intervals through the night following the burning of the boat, teams of guisers visit each dance in turn and entertain the assembled crowds to mimes, playlets, songs and dance routines. It is a sort of roving revue in which it is not difficult to find echoes of the kind of entertainment provided in the medieval burghs of mainland Scotland. For the Guiser Jarl read the Lord of Misrule, the Abbot of Unreason.

As for the Sword Dance of Papa Stour, from whichever source it sprang, it has no present-day counterpart on the mainland of Scotland. However, its links with dances extant in other lands abound. An almost identical form of Sword Dance is regularly performed in the Basque country, on the Franco-Spanish border. And in Morris dancing surviving in England, sword play invariably includes the forming of the intertwined 'star' which is also raised during the Sword Dance of Papa Stour.

It is a dance which teases the dance historian. It seems to be a mixture of Morris, sword dance and mummers' traditions – or, is it such a perfect relic that it can be taken as evidence that mummers' plays, Morris dancing and sword dancing are but branches of the same root?

In living memory on the island the performance of the dance was heralded by much preparation. The dance was never performed casually. Always its presentation was an event which required that the audience be in suitably receptive mood. It was most often performed on a date between modern Christmas and Old Yule, at the beginning of January.

A native of Papa Stour, George Peterson, gives this account of performances in the 1930s: 'I vividly remember the atmosphere of rapt attention given to the dance by the isle's folk, old and young alike; the stir of anticipation as the performers marched in with dignity; the thrill as the fiddler struck up the old tune – recalling memories of former times and old dancers now at rest, and the chatter of conversation that resumed after the applause at the end, as concentration relaxed.

'There was no hall and the Dance was done in the school. And an old man would reminisce about the days before the school was built when the Dance was performed in a "vodd" house, unoccupied, or at the home of the renowned fiddler, Johnnie Umphra at the Biggins. He was a person who loved to play, who sought any excuse for a tune. His wife was no whit behindhand in drawing back the chairs and clearing the spacious kitchen end for a dance for "da young anes". All were welcome at any time.

'And here the humble cottage, now roofless and fallen into decay, echoed to the clash of swords and scuff of feet over the earthen floor and the strains of the Sword Dance music; as the glow of the aurora flickered up over the dark sky without, a shower of hail whispered over the thatch, and the distant boom and thunder of the great Atlantic surges troubled the towering ramparts at the back of the island.

'Dear island. Kindly old Papa Stour!'

When one considers that the entire performance of the Sword Dance of Papa Stour in its present form takes little more than fifteen minutes, then it is not unreasonable to suppose the aura of expectation and mystique described was as time-honoured as the dance itself and that the dance was originally of much longer duration. Today the Sword Dance is no longer performed on the island, but the fact that it can still be seen at all is in great measure thanks to two Papa Stour men.

The dance had not been performed for many years when, in 1950, Alexander Johnstone got up a performance for the Viking Congress in Lerwick. He researched among the older men of the island to get the form and movements of the dance accurate. The old music was found.

A member of that team in 1950 was George Peterson, a schoolboy, who today, as a schoolmaster at Brae on Shetland, teaches the Sword Dance of Papa Stour to young Shetlanders, adhering as strictly as he possibly can to the traditions of the dance which tells the story of the Seven Champions of Christendom. The music used is unique, not used for any other dance. It was collected from John Fraser whose family had been the traditional Sword Dance fiddlers for generations back. There is a tune for the 'March On' in duple time and another for the 'Trip' also in duple time. The Sword Dance itself is performed to a tune in triple time, and has a distinctly Scandinavian drone base.

Today's text for the spoken part of the performance is taken from Sir Walter Scott's *The Pirate*. The authority for using these words rests in the acceptance that they are the words exactly as dictated to Sir Walter while on a visit to Shetland with the Scottish Lighthouse Commissioners in the early years of the 19th century.

On the assumption that Scott did take down the words accurately, and because they differ little from two other versions noted around that time, successive performers and rescuers of the dance have little doubt that they are authentic.

Generations of dancers since medieval times must have brought about changes in the dance, but changes only of a peripheral nature. Mr Peterson's boys, for instance, dance with swords fashioned from strip steel instead of straightened herring barrel hoops. And the hilts of their swords are painted to match the coloured bands worn to identify each Champion of Christendom.

Each dancer wears black trousers, a white shirt, black shoes and a band of appropriate colour. These colours are absolutely traditional. St George of England wears a red band diagonally over his shoulder and also a blue rosette to distinguish him as leader. St James of Spain wears a band of light purple. St Denis of France wears gold with a scarlet edging and St Anthony of Italy's band is a light pink. St David of Wales sports deep yellow with a dark green edging. St Patrick wears green and St Andrew wears blue.

Nowadays there is not the 'exuberant and uncouth glee' reported by a 19th-century eye-witness, and, indeed, the dance has probably lost a great deal of pantomime which can be imagined from the words. The boys who perform today are, understandably, not yet of an age to appreciate nor to exploit fully the significance of the words and of the dance, but as George Peterson's earliest pupils have now formed an adult team, the continuation of a very old traditional dance seems assured with the likelihood of a revival of some of its pantomime content.

For the performance the musician stands to the left of the audience, on the performers' right, and the action begins with the entry of St George who bows and declares:

> *Brave gentles all within this boor,* [bower]
> *If ye delight in any sport,*
> *Come see me dance upon this floor.*
> *Then shall I dance in such a sort.*
> *You minstrel man, play me a porte.*

The fiddler plays a specific tune of four bars during which St George holds his sword by hilt and point above his head and performs the Trip – a back shuffle which is a traditional step but which very experienced dancers in the old days augmented into a more spectacular step reminiscent of 'treepling', a step with a fast fluttering, tapping of the feet.

Having bowed once more to the audience, St George then tells them, in rhyme, of his travels in several countries in which he has undertaken feats of strength and been engaged in sword fights but has never been defeated. There is a deal of boasting and bravado about the words which are not difficult to imagine being rendered in comical vein.

> And by the strength of this right hand,
> Once in a day I killed fifteen,
> And left them dead upon the land.
> Therefore brave minstrel do not care
> But play to me a porte most light
> That I no longer do forbear,
> But dance in all these gentles' sight.

The musician plays the Trip again and St George again dances.

> Although my strength makes you abased,
> Brave gentles do not be afraid,
> For here are six champions, with me, staid,
> All by my manhood I have raised.
> Since I have danced I think it's best
> To call my brethren in your sight,
> That I may have a little rest,
> And they may dance with all their might
> And shake their sword of steel so bright
> And show their main strength on this floor,
> For we shall have another bout
> Before we pass out of this boor.
> Therefore, brave minstrel, do not care
> To play to me a porte most light
> That I no longer do forbear,
> But dance in all these gentles' sight.

The fiddler plays the March On — twelve bars of music — and the six Champions enter to an introduction from St George. After he has introduced each in turn he demonstrates to them his challenge which is to dance the Trip. As the dance is performed today each boy does exactly the same back-stepping shuffle but doubtless in former days there would have been some attempt to outdance each other at this point — either earnestly or in jest.

As each comes forward to do his Trip St George introduces him. For example:

> Stout James of Spain, both tried and stour,
> Thine acts are known full well indeed,
> Present thyself within our sight,
> Without either fear or dread.
> Count not for favour or for fied,
> Since of thy acts thou hast been sure;
> Brave James of Spain, I will thee lead,
> To prove thy manhood on this floor.

James comes forward and performs the Trip in imitation of St George who then proceeds with the remainder of his introductions, ending with St Andrew. With each saint, allusions are made to brave deeds and actions but always with a slight suggestion of poking fun – except in the case of St Andrew:

> *Thou kindly Scotsman, come thou here,*
> *Thy name is Andrew of Fair Scotland*
> *Draw out thy sword that is most clear,*
> *Fight for thy King with thy right hand;*
> *Fight for thy King with all thy heart;*
> *And then, for to confirm his band,*
> *Make all his enemies to smart.*

The Champions all introduced, the Sword Dance proper begins. St George and the Champions strike swords, step over them, pass them overhead, form a steel circle by holding the swords by hilt and point. In the course of the dance – which is to the accompaniment of a tune of twelve bars repeated – they form a spiral, a clew, and in climax a 'star' is formed by interlocking the swords. This star is held aloft by each in turn.

The star is pulled apart and as the Champions line up, sword on shoulder, behind St George, he speaks the Epilogue:

> *Mars does rule he bends his brows*
> *He makes us all aghast*
> *After the few hours that we stay here,*
> *Venus will rule at last.*
> *Farewell, farewell, brave gentles all*
> *That herein do remain,*
> *We wish you health and happiness*
> *Till we return again.*

In the words of the introductions we can find much to suggest the original manner in which the dance was performed. Italy's representative is treated by St George as something of a buffoon. David of Wales, waiting to come forward to do his Trip, would probably have made much of the allusion to his habit of cleaving things in 'twa at a stroke'.

It is easy to imagine the actions from the words. Note, too, the show biz of keeping St Andrew till last! When the play was originally, as suspected, performed on mainland Scotland, Andrew would have had little to do in the way of showing off besides walking about serenely, acknowledging the chauvinistic applause – the perfect prelude, in fact, to the Sword Dance which begins immediately afterwards.

The Sword Dance of Papa Stour affords us a sample of a kind

of dancing and play acting largely unknown on the mainland since the banning of May Games and the like in the 16th century. It is certainly a direct ancestor of the masques so beloved of the Stewart kings and queens.

The remoteness of Papa Stour ensured the survival of the Sword Dance and from a nearby island comes another survivor of an old dance form – the Foula Reel which blends some Scottish influence with an ancient Scandinavian weaving dance. There is much in the Foula Reel which is reminiscent of a children's playground game and its simple formations mark it out as a very early dance indeed.

Dances which tell a story without words belong to earliest times. Pantomime figured greatly in medieval dancing, and today's most familiar survivor of this form of dancing in Scotland is to be found in the children's playground game of Bee Baw Babbity or Babbity Bowser, known as a ring dance and 'cushion' dance for centuries.

As the game is played today, one of the number is selected to stand in the centre of the ring while the others circle round singing. This version is from east Fife:

Bee baw babbity, babbity, babbity,
Bee baw babbity, kiss a bonny wee lassie/laddie.
Kneel down and kiss the ground, kiss the ground, kiss the ground,
Kneel down and kiss the ground, kiss a bonny wee lassie/laddie.
I widna hae a lassie/laddie o, lassie o, lassie o,
I widna hae a lassie/laddie o, I'd rather have a wee laddie/lassie.

The very last 'lassie' or 'laddie' is repeated over and over until the boy or girl in the middle has chosen someone in the circle to be kissed, who in turn becomes the one in the middle.

Bee Baw Babbity in the form of Babbity Bowster is one of the earliest named of all Scottish dances. The bowster of the title was the bolster or cushion on which the central figure knelt. The original form of the dance was a rather more complicated business of partners kneeling together on the cushion to kiss, with the ladies selecting partners by dropping a handkerchief beside the man of their choice – an action which is found today in another playground game, 'I sent a letter to my love, and on the way I dropped it'. Babbity Bowster, the cushion dance, was an important part of wedding celebrations until comparatively recent times in Scotland.

Many of the oldest ballads in the language have a recurrent line or chorus which suggests to some historians a link between ballads and dancing. It is easy to imagine a repeated word like

'benorie, benorie' or a phrase such as 'in this New Yeir, in this
New Yeir' being chanted as a chorus by a ring of dancers round
a central miming figure. The 'carols' and 'chorees', mentioned
frequently in 14th- and 15th-century burgh records, refer to
processional or ring dances.

Another carefully recorded early dance, from the North West
and the Hebrides, is *Cath nan Coileach*, The Reeling of the Cocks,
which is for two couples and contains movements representing
the antics of fighting cocks. Other reels from the same region,
performed until the middle of the last century, had movements
imitating ducks and the courtship ceremonies at the lek of
blackcock – the display ground where these birds congregate.
Such dances were evidently relics of a strong tradition of
pantomime dances which had begun not as dance movements
worked out to a tune but as pieces of folk pantomime which
contained much 'reeland' or reeling.

There are several early references to reeling which became the
term applied to the action of setting to and turning partners and
forming figures of eight. To reel, which shouldn't be confused with
reel-time, meant, from earliest times, to get together and dance.

One last indication of the popularity of pantomime dances is
found in early Scottish poems and from these, too, come the
evidence that individuals could become renowned in a
community for their performances in these dances. For instance
in the 15th-century ballad, *Peblis to the Play*, we read:

> With that Will Swane came sweatand out,
> Ane meikle miller man;
> 'Gif I sall dance have done, lat see,
> Blaw up the bagpipe than!
> The schamous dance I maun begin;
> I trow it sall not pane.'
> So heavily he hochit about,
> To see him, Lord, as they ran,
>   That tide,
> Of Peblis to the play.
>
> They gadderit out of the toun,
> And nearer him they dreuch;
> And bade gife the danceris room;
> Will Swane makis wonder teuch . . .

In spite of the difficulty of old Scots, the roistering intent of it
all is very clear. And Will Swane 'hoching' heavily about
imitating a salmon with, no doubt, a great deal of twisting and
leaping is a further tantalizing glimpse of a common form of

dance long gone. Gone, that is, unless the next time you do an Eightsome Reel you half close your eyes as you watch the antics of the men as they take their turn to be in the centre of the ring.

Will Swane has descendants in every ballroom and village hall!

2
THE STEWART LEGACY

From James I to James VI, all the Stewart kings of Scotland came to their inheritance and titles as small children. The consequence to the common folk was a couple of centuries of fending off English take-over bids and embroilment in the baronial struggles for ascendancy by a succession of regents, then, when the king finally came to the throne in his own right, being subjected to often brief, and sometimes stormy, reigns which ended, with one exception, in tragedy.

At a time when the remainder of Europe was awakening to the glories of a cultural and spiritual Renaissance, the Scots would not have been even a tributary of the European mainstream had it not been for a series of dynastic marriages and the strangely durable Auld Alliance with France.

Not one of Scotland's kings called James took a Scottish queen. The First and Fourth took English brides. The Third and Sixth fetched princesses home from Denmark. The Second and Fifth made French alliances. For almost two hundred years Scotland had a variety of foreign court influences, each in its turn affecting the life of Lowland Scotland in general and of the city of Edinburgh in particular.

But the most important influence was that of the Auld Alliance which had been formalized, rather surprisingly, by King John Balliol in 1295. 'Surprisingly', since Balliol's rule in Scotland had been almost entirely dependent upon his vassalage to Edward I of England, Hammer of the Scots. Scottish kings before had allied with the French. The Alexanders II and III had both married French wives – it was in his determination to get back to St Andrews and his beloved Queen Yolande de Dreux that Alexander III had risked and broken his neck along the shore at Kinghorn in Fife in 1286. The Wars of Independence and Succession which followed all involved patriotic Scottish claimants to the throne, each with Norman/French names – Comyn, Balliol, de Brus.

Succeeding years saw a strengthening of the links as the Anglo-French Hundred Years War pointed up the usefulness to France of a Scottish ally who could be guaranteed to make it difficult for England to devote its entire energies to defeating

France. Scotland had its use as a gadfly – a cleg, willing to draw English blood from the rear!

Thousands of Scottish troops served over the centuries in the armies of France. A force of Scots helped Joan of Arc to lift the Siege of Orléans, in 1429, which marked the turning of the tide of the Hundred Years War in France's favour and led to the eventual surrender by the English of their French territories. The kings of France came to have a close bodyguard of which they were extremely proud – La Garde Ecossaise. And in return for services rendered, French soldiers were often sent to bolster the Scottish army.

The Auld Alliance was renewed several times over the centuries by treaty. But, in human terms, bits of paper with seals and signatures are not required to reinforce indissoluble bonds between peoples.

Even today, Lowland Scotland still reflects the endurance of the Alliance and the legacy of the French who lived there in language, ways with food, sweetmeats, and in mannerisms. The narrow 'oo' sound in east coast speech is an echo of the French tongue. Things French are so much a part of Lowland Scottish life that the Scots themselves are mostly unaware of the Frenchness. Large plates are ashets (*assiettes*). Clothes can be tashed (*tacher* to soil) by rain which cundies (*conduits*) can't remove fast enough. A Scot might eat a shortbread petticoat tail not knowing that it got its name from a *petite galette* which is a broad, thin cake or biscuit. Or he might sit down to Scottish hotchpotch, vegetable soup, and not know he was partaking of the French *hochepot*. And in Lowland Scotland, nice folk are 'douce', hard folk are 'dour'. The polite are 'genteel'.

One lasting sociological effect of the Auld Alliance in the Middle Ages is that, because it affected only Lowland Scotland in any great measure, it served to underscore the already sharp differences between the cultures and lives of the Highland and the Lowland Scot.

The French influence was, and remains, at its strongest on the east coast and in the central southern belt, from the Moray coast to the Borders, particularly in Fife and around Edinburgh. And as the French influenced the language, the architecture, the manners of the city and burgh folk, they naturally influenced the music and dance.

Despite all the internal upheavals and wars of preceding reigns, by James IV's time, at the end of the 15th into the beginning of the 16th century, the country was enjoying an unprecedented era of expansion and prosperity when the Renaissance came to Scotland. Royal residences which had always been fortress castles were rebuilt as palaces. They retained their strategic sites but bright walls of windows appeared within the old battlements. And there was room now for gardens and bowers for Her Majesty's enjoyment.

James IV married, in 1503, Margaret Tudor, the daughter of Henry VII of England and sister of the man who would become Henry VIII. The marriage, called the Union of the Thistle and the Rose, brought with it hopes for peace at last between England and Scotland. It did eventually provide just that – a hundred years later, in 1603, when Margaret and James's great-grandson, James VI, succeeded Elizabeth Tudor and the Union of the Thistle and the Rose became the Union of the Crowns.

But that was an unforeseeable future event, though devoutly hoped for, when James IV summoned girls to dance at his wedding and ordered the musicians and mummers to be paid by the Lord High Treasurer. And on the birth of a royal prince, in 1507, it is recorded that payment was made to one Guillian 'for the making of a dance'. Makers of dances to Royal Command were paid often and well in James's time.

The royal years were marked by a series of Festivals and Progresses round the realm – or as much of it as could provide suitable housing for a king and his retinue.

The Christmas season, the King's Yule, might be celebrated with daily Masses and evenings of mummers and dances at Holyrood or Linlithgow. Spring and Beltane feasts were held where there was decent hunting, in the north at Huntly or in Fife, with a day's sport easily and pleasantly rounded off in dining and dancing or watching the Morris men in blackface capering around.

In the early years of the 16th century the favourite social dances – dances for which people took partners and performed together as opposed to dances they watched only – were branles and basse dances.

The basse dances were couple dances which had originated in the French countryside, it is believed, and as they became popular throughout most of Western Europe, they developed regional variations. By the early 15th century basse dances had become the dances of the aristocracy in every court.

Michiel Toulouse, a 15th-century French writer on dancing, suggests that the term 'basse' meaning 'low' was associated with these dances because of their lowly peasant origins rather than their low steps (as opposed to the high leaping of other popular court dances).

In 1521 Robert Coplande published in London *The manner of dauncynge bace daunces* as a sort of appendix to a scholar's textbook. A preface to a 20th-century edition of this work suggests that from its date, the year following the magnificent Field of the Cloth of Gold meeting between Henry VIII and Francis I of France, it was an attempt by the publisher to capitalize on the current popularity in England of French manners and modes. (Because of the Auld Alliance with the French, it is likely that the French style of basse dances would have been well known in Scotland long before this.)

Coplande's chapter on 'Bace daunces' is a translation, at times very literal, from the French. Without preamble it begins: 'For to dance any Bace dance there behoveth four paces, that is to wit, single, double, reprise and branle. And ye ought first to make reverence toward the lady, and then make two singles, one double, a reprise and a branle. And this rule ye ought alway to keep at the beginning as it is said.'

An explanation follows of how dance instructions are set down, and the dancer is advised to 'know the number of notes of every Bace dance, and the paces after the measure of the notes'. Know your tune, in other words, and fit the steps of the dance accordingly.

Much emphasis is given in the chapter to 'raising the body' – conveying that the dancer is meant to spring lightly – something the Scots loved to do in their native reels.

'Branle steps' are included in the instructions, but the branle was itself a popular dance which also had regional variations like the basse dance, and Coplande's instruction for 'Branle steps' may be interpreted as the travelling step used in the branle dance.

After James IV's untimely end at Flodden, in 1513, Scotland again had an infant king. The Queen Mother, Margaret, married the ambitious Earl of Angus and the country was plunged into another power struggle.

Ordinary folk, though, seem to have found occasion to dance, since a list of dances has survived in the anonymous poem of the period, *Cockelbie's Sow*.

Cockelbie's Sow tells the story of the sale of a pig, how the three pennies it earned were spent and the results of spending them. The poet evidently loved lists. There are lists of guests at a harlot's table, giving a marvellous roll-call of the trades and professions of the time and, for the dancer's delectation, a list of the dances danced by sundry folk, and the manner of their dancing:

> *Some trottit Tras and Trenas*
> *Some balterit the Bass,*
> *Some Perdony, some Trolly Lolly,*

> *Some Cock craw thou whill day,*
> *Taysbank and Terway.*
> *Some Lincolne some Lindsay,*
> *Some Jolly Leman daws it not day.*
> *Some beckit, some bingit,*
> *Some crackit, some cringit,*
> *Some movit Most Mak Revell,*
> *Some Maister Pier de Couzate,*
> *And other some in consate*
> *Some Ourfute, some Orliance,*
> *Some Rusty Bully with a bek,*
> *And Every Note in Other's neck.*

Not only a variety of titles but of dancing styles and a mixture of ring dances, solo dances, basse dances. 'Orliance' is certainly a Scottish corruption of a tune of that time called Orléans. 'Rusty Bully', too, is a corruption of 'Roti, Bolli, Joyeux', a very early longways country dance.

Whoever the writer was, he gave us in *Cockelbie's Sow* a catalogue of the seeds, at least, of our social dances.

All the dance titles in the poem are evidence of dances known in Scotland at the time of writing. Poets of popular ballads made much use of familiar, everyday images and names when looking for a wide success. The subjects they treated had to be well known to their intended readers and listeners. Thus it is not mere supposition that leads to the claim that such dances were the popular dancing at the beginning of the 16th century.

James V came to power in 1524 following the governorship of his uncle the Duke of Albany. He, the Duke, was in truth more French than Scottish – not an uncommon feature of the Scottish aristocracy thanks to the Auld Alliance.

Much of what has been cited as evidence of French influence is often credited to Mary Queen of Scots' reign later in the century but it is to this earlier era that we must look for the French influences which were most lasting upon our culture and our dancing – particularly our social dancing. We need look back, in fact, no farther than to the reign of Mary's father James V and the regency of her French mother, James's second wife, Mary of Guise.

Because of the French influence brought to bear under his uncle's governorship, when the time came for James V to look for a wife, a good French marriage was the first consideration. And in 1537 James married Madeleine, daughter of Francis I, the great Renaissance King of France. Tragically, Madeleine survived but a few brief weeks after her arrival in Scotland.

James's second marriage took place the following year to the

23-year-old widow of Francis d'Orléans, Duc de Longueville.
The Duchesse, had been before her marriage to Francis, Marie de
Guise, a daughter of the power-hungry Duc de Guise.

James, in spite of his permanently roving eye, did all that was
in his power to make Marie's life in Scotland more tolerable.
Stirling Castle and Linlithgow Palace were renovated in a style
less military, more pleasantly domestic. Falkland Palace in the
shadow of the Lomond Hills in Fife was rebuilt in the French
style. It could be transported stone by stone to the banks of the
Loire and be in no way out of place there. This became the
favourite royal hunting lodge.

Marie surrounded herself not only with French things but
with French people. Her retinue was considerable in size, and
wholly French. It was to remain so, with regular additions from
France, for more than twenty years.

At the beginning of the marriage all went well for James and
Marie. A son was born, assuring the Stewart dynasty in
Scotland. But suddenly, in 1541, the prince died a few days
after the stillbirth of a second son. The parents, and the nation,
were desolate.

But there was hope yet. Marie and James were young – there
would be more children and in the spring of 1542 Marie found
herself again with child. General rejoicing and celebrations with
dancing were, however, tempered by trouble with the English,
which came to a head later in the year in November with the
rout of the Scottish army at Solway Moss. James went to
Falkland Palace where he gave way utterly to despair – a despair
intensified rather than alleviated when news was brought to
him early in December of the birth of his daughter, Mary. A few
days later, James turned his face to the wall and died, and the
baby, Mary, was Queen of Scots. Nineteen years were to pass
however, before the little queen came to her throne.

Her childhood and growing-up were spent in France, while
her mother Marie, with the active support of the French court
and the Guise uncles, not to mention a considerable French army,
took over as Regent of Scotland.

That French army – between seven and eight thousand strong
– remained in Scotland for ten years. In a small country with a
very small population it is not possible that a group of
foreigners in such number and over such a period of time could
leave no trace of occupation. Of course they did – traces a-plenty,
and much that abides. Place names, surnames, songs and dances.

We know about the dances thanks to a list in a piece of protest
literature printed in 1549. Much has been conjectured about the
authorship of *The Complaynt of Scotland* which appeared when
the country was at yet another low ebb. There were two foreign

armies on Scottish soil – French and English. The Lowlands of Scotland had been laid waste by Henry VIII's troops in the attempted Rough Wooing for the promise of the young queen in marriage to his infant son.

Discontent against the debauched Roman religious order was gathering strength. Because of his reforming activities, John Knox was held prisoner in France between 1547 and 1549.

There was plenty to make 'complaynt' about. The writer draws attention to the plight of his country and, in a strange series of visions and dreams, describes an idyllic countryside as it might be, given peace and good government. And, in the way of popular pamphleteers, he uses images and names which would have been very familiar to his readers in order to make the greatest impact upon them.

He visualizes shepherds and their wives singing and dancing in a ring. They dance to the accompaniment of eight musicians – bagpipes, jews harp, an assortment of woodwinds and a fiddle.

'I beheld never a more delectable recreation,' declares the writer as he describes the dancing.

It began with 'two beks and with a kiss', two bows and a kiss. Visitors to these shores in the 16th century commented on the amount of kissing which went on. It was the accepted salutation in those days, and for a dance to start with a kiss between partners would be considered nothing out of the ordinary. Time or a chord was allowed at the beginning and the end of a dance for the kiss. Nowadays our bow and curtsey are simply shadows of this former practice.

The dancing which followed the kissing in *The Complaynt* was a vision of perfection.

'Euripides, Juvenal, Perseus, Horace, nor none of the satyric poets had they moved their bodies as they pronounced their tragedies, would have kept more geometrical measure than these shepherds did in their dancing. It was a celestial recreation to behold their light leaping, gambolling, striding backwards and forwards, dancing Basse dances, Pavans, Galliards, Turdions, Brawls and Branles, Buffons, with many other light dances, too many to mention.

'Yet nonetheless I shall rehearse as many as I can recall.'

There follows a list of dances which indicates that the common folk must have known at least of the existence of these dances as well as the French pavans, galliards and turdions, if the pamphlet was to pack any sort of a punch. From the considerable list, here are some of the names: All Christian Men, The North of Scotland, Hunt's Up, The Gossip's Dance, The Spade, The Flail, Robin Hood, the Deid Dance, John Armstrong's Dance.

All Christian Men sounds like the title of a carol, choree or ring dance, and the dance, taking its name from the tune, may have been a remnant from a mummers' play performed at some Christian festival. This is conjecture, but a considerable number of Christmas and other carols which are still sung have repeated choruses and a distinct dance rhythm. Certainly, Robin Hood would be a dance with festival and ballad origins.

John Armstrong, the border riever who was hanged in the reign of James V, is the subject of a celebrated ballad. Such a ballad no doubt gave rise to a dance full of mime and action. John Armstrong's Dance may well have shown the kicking and turning reminiscent of a man's death throes on the gallows – gruesome to our generation, but acceptable in former times.

One title, Come Kytil me Nakit, Wantonly, may have been a branle performed to a bawdy song tune.

The Deid Dance was a variation of a dance found all over Europe: the Dance of Death full of movement and mime, with origins deep in history.

The Flail and The Spade were also dances with pantomime, a form which survived well into the 19th century in the outer isles of Scotland. A modern interpretation of this style of dance is The Hebridean Weaving Lilt. The stamping of the feet and the steps in this dance are quite unlike any other performed nowadays in Scotland, though they can be seen in Scandinavian dancing. The stamping signifies the passing of a length of cloth from hand to hand around a table to be thumped thereon to 'wauk' the cloth – a pre-shrinking process.

'Basse Dances, Pavans, Galliards, Turdions, Brawls and Branles, Buffons . . . Basse dances were country dances to popular melodies, which came into social use via the court. They may have been the first formalized couple dances with their own steps, their own formations, not unlike the modern Gay Gordons, although the use of the arms in that dance makes it a close relative of the galliard and the allemande.

Pavans were couple dances in the style of a basse dance but with a deal of courtliness, so courtly, indeed, that they could be danced with cloak and sword, according to one contemporary authority. Pavan music played twice as fast made the rhythm of a basse dance. On a dance programme pavans would be followed by the livelier turdion and galliard to give variety.

Buffons were a form of sword dance in the style of the Sword Dance of Papa Stour, with interlocking swords and mock sword play. They were principally associated with mummers' plays and, latterly in Scotland, with trades' guilds.

Brawls and branles – the author lists them separately in The Complaynt – were, in fact, two names for the same dance. That word 'brawl' which turns up regularly in 15th- and 16th-century poetry and prose – 'whereof a thousand brawls he doth compound' – means the dancing of brawls or branles and has nothing to do with fist-fighting. A branle was a round-the-room couple dance. As branles had gained in popularity they, like basse dances, had developed regional and national characteristics. There were Branles de Champagne, Branles de Poitou and there was one branle of particular interest to us, the Branle d'Ecosse, the Scottish Branle.

The Branle d'Ecosse is well documented in a remarkable book which was produced in France in 1588 by Thoinot Arbeau, pseudonym of a Canon of Langres. Entitled the *Orchésographie*, it contains the author's system of choreography, his ideas on the uses of military music, as well as etiquette and dance instruction.

The book takes the form of a conversation between Capriol, a young man who wishes to learn the courtly arts, and Arbeau, the dancing master, author of the volume. It contains a host of interesting observations in the guise of answers to gauche questions.

The martial arts are mentioned, as is the use of drum-beat rhythm in military drill. With a tantalizingly brief reference to martial dancing he goes into considerable detail about the use of an increased drum rhythm to heighten the excitement of men being led into battle.

Writing of basse dances, Arbeau states: 'The basse dance has been out of date some forty or fifty years, but I foresee that wise and dignified matrons will restore it to fashion as being a type of dance full of virtue and decorum.' This, written in 1588, indicated that the fashion for the dance in France had passed between 1538 and 1548 – at about the same time as *The Complaynt* was being compiled.

In 1547, Henry II came to the French throne and it was his wife Catherine de Medici who introduced from Italy a more formal, more 'artistic' series of balletic dance forms into the French court. Perhaps Arbeau's wish for the return of the popularity of basse dances reflected a need to get back to simpler, more social dances.

In the reign of Henry and Catherine de Medici, branles became extremely popular. From some of their titles it has been suggested that they may have included an element of mime, some of it bawdy. This may also be a reason for Arbeau's wish to get back to the basse dancing of earlier times 'full of virtue and decorum'.

But too much importance must not be placed on titles since they were almost invariably songs or airs to which dances had become attached. Arbeau makes it quite clear that the number of

movements employed in dancing a branle was adjusted to suit
the length of the tune. The tune came first – and along with
the tune, a title which was then attached to the dance.

As for dancing basse dances, branles, and the rest, Arbeau
favours stateliness and courtesy. He repeats on several occasions
that a man ought to dance in such a way as to be able to regard
his partner. For example, in making the 'reverence' at the
beginning of the dance, he says that it should be done with the
right foot, enabling one to turn towards the damsel 'and throw
her a courteous glance'. He follows with a description of some
branle steps interspersed with remarks such as, 'to the right
again with a discreetly tender sidelong glance at the damsel',
and, 'you must be careful not to take strides that suggest you
wish to measure the length of the hall, as the damsel who is your
partner cannot, with decency, take such long steps'.

The progression of basse dances, branles, galliards and the
rest was round the room, and the dimension of movements
forward and back between partners was highly dependent upon
how crowded the room was.

Certain knowledge was necessary on the part of the
participants as they were expected to be thoroughly conversant
with the basic dance steps and formations. And one can imagine
the men before mirrors practising their sidelong glances!

Arbeau writes: 'When one knows the steps and movements
of one pavan and one common basse dance one can dance all the
others. Because, although the melodies differ, and they may be
either sung or played, they all have the same number of bars.
And you will note that the steps of the coranto must be
executed with a spring which is not the case in the pavan or the
basse dance.' Social dancing, then, had become an orderly matter
of fitting steps to tunes, under the guidance of a dancing master
and musician.

Couple dancing was a mixture of rural dances and dances of
more courtly origin, each performed in succession to give a
varied programme. 'Folk' dancing had gone up in the world,
into the ballrooms – to stay there, in Scotland, at least. And
this mixture of very formal court dances, galliards, pavans,
corantos with the less formal introductions from the countryside,
branles and basse dances, was the dancing of the Scottish court
in the 16th century.

Outside the court, the ring dances, reels and ceremonial
dances continued. But Scotland is a small country. The distance,
physical and social, between the court and lesser subjects,
between the royal palaces and the closes and farm towns, was
never so wide as in larger countries with greater concentrations
of population. What happened at court, court manners and

modes, filtered down fairly quickly through the various strata of Scottish society.

Burgh merchants' homes were, by the 16th century, reasonably comfortably decorated and well appointed. Their wives wore imported, costly silks and hung Arras tapestries on the walls of their homes – homes with glazed windows and pewter tableware. And, in imitation, the servants would do their utmost to afford at least one set of special clothes for special days.

If clothes and manners were imitated, then so were the songs and dances. Galliards, pavans and the like would be known to the populace at large, even if they did prefer the older native forms of dancing. And there's little doubt that it was very early in the history of dance in Scotland that the two forms of dancing, the courtly and the native, became intertwined.

More than one visitor to the country at that time commented on the innate gaiety and liveliness of the people in spite of their surroundings. The Scots have always loved to dance.

Whether the author of *The Complaynt of Scotland* considered the return of Mary Queen of Scots to this country, in 1561, as any solution to Scottish troubles is not recorded. But she certainly was a vision of loveliness. Her childhood and teenage years had been spent in the splendour of the homes of her Guise grandparents and uncles in the French court where she was the delight of poets for her matchless beauty and the joy of the courtiers for her elegance and charm. Mary's early life in France had been a succession of pleasures, progressions from château to château, often in company with the elegant Diane de Poitiers, mistress of the king. This life was a far and gentle cry from the court that awaited Mary in her northern kingdom. Perhaps it was as well that she was afforded a sudden view of life's hardness and disappointments in the swift series of events which were the prelude to her return to Scotland.

Her father-in-law, Henry II of France, died suddenly, and foolishly, while taking part in a tournament in 1559. Her husband, the fifteen-year-old Dauphin, became Francis II of France – with the Guise uncles making certain that they were the real power in the land. But within a few months Francis II was dead, and the Guise uncles' dreams of absolute power were shattered. Mary, as Queen of Scots, dowager of France and considered in all Catholic countries to be the rightful Queen of England, was just too much of a potential rival for power for the comfort of Catherine de Medici, widow of Henry II.

Meanwhile, in Scotland over the past ten years, Mary's mother, Marie de Guise, had been embroiled in a growing threat of civil war between the Protestant Lords and those who remained loyal to the old faith which had the support of Marie and her French court advisers.

The threat became reality and bitter civil war was fought in 1559 and 1560. The Lords of the Congregation, as the leading Protestants were known, prevailed, fortified by the preaching of Knox returned from imprisonment in France via Geneva and Reformed England. They were supported too by the mass of the people sick of an over-fat clergy in a poverty-stricken land.

Marie, defeated, and heartily sick of the constant strife and the hectoring of Knox, was mortally ill and collapsed and died in Edinburgh Castle in 1560. It was decided that the widowed Mary in France should return home, and home she came to a cold, northern country in the August of the following year, 1561. Home, to a Protestant state – and she a Catholic Queen.

It is in no small measure due to Mary's force of character, her striking beauty, her love of people and her willingness to try to be wise and rule well, that the outset of her reign was relatively happy.

Masques and dances were held to honour her safe arrival – though she may ruefully have contrasted the Scottish notion of a suitable greeting with the French way of doing things.

One notable contribution to the welcoming ceremonials in Edinburgh was her greeting from fifty townsmen, their arms and legs blackened, their faces covered in black masks and all garbed in yellow taffeta. The blacking of faces was very much part of the Morris and guising traditions.

Thoinot Arbeau in his *Orchésographie* recalls a blackface dancer when he was a young man, about 1540. He wrote: 'In fashionable society when I was young, a small boy, his face daubed with black and his forehead swathed in a white and yellow kerchief, would make an appearance after supper. He wore leggings covered with little bells and performed a morris, wherein he advanced the length of the room, made a kind of passage and then moving backwards retraced his steps to the place from whence he started. Then he executed a new passage and he continued thus making various passages which delighted the spectators.'

Having spent so much of her life in France growing up in the court whose chief entertainment was dancing, Mary would have had considerable knowledge of this kind of blackface presentation and also of the more formal kind of masque which was coming into vogue.

Fat little Edinburgh bairns got up as angels and reading psalms from the top of triumphal arches, not to mention the braying of several hundred ill-assorted musical instruments, must have been a poor substitute for the glories of masques devised under Catherine de Medici's instruction.

Queen Catherine is credited not only with the popularizing of the formal masque and making it an essential part of French court life, but she is also said to have been directly responsible for the introduction to France of the high-leaping, Italian style of court dancing. Though, when the French got their feet to that style of dancing, they soon made it more elegant and closer to the floor, and trimmed it of its twisting and leaping. This more elegant, less acrobatic dancing was the style which Mary learned.

(The leaping, high-stepping Italian style went, incidentally, direct to England from Italy, by-passing the moderating French court influence, to be danced at Elizabeth's court with sometimes literally leg-breaking energy!)

In Compan's *Dictionnaire de Danse*, in 1787, the author credits Catherine de Medici with the enlivening of the court balls, giving these celebrations a certain style which left an 'enduring happy memory' and gave rise to the magnificence of the balls held at Versailles by Louis XIV a century later. Balls at Catherine's court always began with a branle led by the chief guests, usually the king and queen.

This, then, was the style of dancing and entertainment to which Mary had been accustomed when she came to live at Holyrood, that turreted Renaissance palace renovated and much extended by her father. There she was to discover in all too short a time that the only similarity between her old life and her new lay in the appearance of that palace and of her favourite at Falkland. But for the moment there was fun, festivities – and the ever-watchful eyes of John Knox who was biding his time and holding his tongue, though not for much longer.

When Queen Mary came home she was barely nineteen years old. John Knox was a powerful, life-hardened 47-year-old whose dancing days were surely done. In more senses than one he had arrived in advance of Mary. He was already the renowned religious leader of the Scottish Reformation, the man who, above all others, had come to be identified with the steering of the ancient kingdom along new paths of sternly-imposed righteousness.

When Mary arrived, John Knox was having his heyday. He was supreme, his word the nearest thing to law the country had heard since before the regency of Marie de Guise. With Knox's assistance, the followers of the new religion were almost invariably able to find scriptural backing for pulling down 'graven images' – throwing out the church organs and dismantling all that was, however vaguely, associated with the old Catholic order.

Dancing, he found to his evident dismay, was something he was unable to condemn outright, 'albeit in the Scriptures I found no praise of it'. He also found it more expedient to bide his time rather than condemn immediately his young Catholic sovereign.

Mary had captured the hearts of the Edinburgh mob, to whom she seemed, as they jostled around her in her first days at Holyrood, the very epitome of how a story-book Queen should be. To a people short on story-books and short on laughter and lightheartedness, Mary must have presented a magical figure.

Life had taught Knox not a few lessons, one of which was how to wait. He knew the fickleness of crowds and this mob pressing round the windows of Holyrood to catch a glimpse of their Queen at play was likely to prove as fickle as any other. He was content to allow Mary to be the people's darling for a time if only because he had the supreme satisfaction of knowing God was on the side of the just – of John Knox.

'The face of heaven,' he wrote in his *History of the Reformation*, 'at the time of her arrival, did manifestly proclaim what comfort was brought unto this country with her, to wit, sorrow, dolour, darkness and all impiety; for in the memory of man, there had never been seen, on that day of the year, a more dolorous face of heaven, than at her arrival . . . the sun was not seen to shine for two days before, nor for two days after. That forewarning gave God unto us; but alas the most part were blind.' Knox, though, meant to prove he wasn't among the blind. In fact, he was on permanent watch for the false move, the stumble that would bring to an end this honeymoon period between the Catholic Queen and her people.

Meantime, the crowd was gathering each day and night at the Canongate end of the Royal Mile, pressing in on the palace, eagerly noting the comings and goings, catching a glimpse from time to time of revellers decked for a masque and dancers enjoying their branles, turdions, galliards, and the like. Story-book stuff, and about as durable.

Sour notes, false steps followed and in a very short time John Knox got his chance to confront his queen. His main platform for attack upon Mary and her court was his pulpit at St Giles'. There he inveighed against them regularly and was called, eventually, to Holyrood to explain himself.

It is evident from Knox's own account of their meetings that he felt he got nowhere with this shrewd young woman. What is more he thought her two-faced, putting on a serious manner for the benefit of her Council, playing 'the hypocrite in full perfection; but as soon as ever her French fillocks [silly young girls] fiddlers and others of that band, got the house alone, there might have been seen skipping [dancing] not very comely for honest women'.

Dances considered 'not very comely' for the common folk were banned in Edinburgh in 1561. These were the dances associated with the May Games, the Robin Hood dances. The ordinary folk were thereby denied one of their sources of fairly innocent amusement and from about this time onwards, with the encouragement of the new clergy, attempts were made throughout the country to suppress all kinds of public dance celebrations. Not, however, with immediate success as repeated finings, punishments, and renewed attempts to enforce the new laws show in the fifty years following.

The Scottish people loved to dance and couldn't associate dancing entirely with the ways of the old religion in their minds – it was something they had done outwith the old church, even if some of their celebrations had been connected with it. Dancing was in the blood and it was going to take more than just a Reformation to purge it.

There can be little doubt that had there been a single word against dancing contained in either the Old or New Testament, Scottish dancing would have gone the way of the painted statues, the organs and everything else considered idolatrous or to pertain to the old ways.

But dancing survived, particularly strongly in places where the Reformation did not bite quite so deeply – in parts of Perthshire and on the east coast north of the Tay. The Kirk had to learn to allow a certain amount of dancing on high days and holidays. Pious Calvinism and festive dancing stepped it out together within well-defined bounds of decorum, for many years following the Reformation – but never on a Sunday!

There was to be 'no dauncing in time of sermon' and no dancing in the churchyards. The punishments for breaking these rules were various and harsh, and imposed often enough to make it clear that such times and places of dancing must have been part of the people's tradition.

Dancing at particular celebrations such as Beltane and Yule was strictly overseen by the Kirk and Town Councils and such festivities came under increasing censure and attack until they all but died out.

Considering all the facets of her character, her supreme wish to rule her country wisely, her wish to worship God in her own way and to allow her subjects to get on peaceably with their own form of worship, it is highly unlikely that Mary Queen of Scots and her court danced, as Knox believed, till past midnight in celebration of the news of the massacre of French Protestants at Vassy in 1562. To Knox, though, this rumour, seemed a heaven-sent chance to let loose from the pulpit in St Giles' the full force of his invective and wrath against those 'skippers, dancers and dalliers with dames' at Holyrood. Had not the head of the Baptist been the reward of Salome's dancing?

When Mary heard of all this she was outraged. Knox was summoned once more to Holyrood to explain himself. He repeated his sermon to her face.

'Of dancing Madam, I said that, albeit in the Scriptures I found no praise of it, and in profane writers that it is termed the gesture rather of those that are mad and in frenzy than of sober men; yet do I not utterly condemn it, providing that two vices be avoided. Firstly, the principal vocation of those that use that exercise must not be neglected for the pleasure of dancing; secondly, they may not dance, as did the Philistines their fathers, for the pleasure that they take in the displeasure of God's people. If they do either, they shall receive the reward of dancers, and that will be to drink in hell, unless they speedily repent, and so shall God turn their mirth into sudden sorrow.'

Poor Mary! 'Maister Knox,' she wrote, 'is so hard on us we have laid aside much of our dancing . . .' Hard indeed for a queen who not only loved to dance but whose contemporaries described her as doing so with a deal of grace and elegance.

In England there was also a queen who loved to dance – Elizabeth Tudor. Sir James Melville, who was Mary's emissary to Elizabeth's court in 1564, found his diplomacy under its severest test when Elizabeth pressed him to compare her with the Queen of Scots. The colour of their hair? Their size? Their musicianship? Did she play music well? demanded Elizabeth of Melville.

Replied Melville, in the epitome of the diplomatic answer, 'Reasonable for a Queen'!

As for dancing, the Queen of Scots danced 'not so high' as the Queen of England, who danced so much in the Italian style that she was known as the Florentine. It might not have amused Elizabeth to learn that her dancing was so well known that it found its way into a book for the education of young men, published in France in 1728, in which the opinion was given that she danced and sang too well to have been chaste!

Sadly, Mary's dancing days were not to last as long as Elizabeth's. In Mary's remaining years of feuds, flights and final imprisonment and execution, there is no talk of dancing among Mary and her faithful retinue. But she did leave her mark upon dancing, in that in a very brief time, 1561–7, she and her court set the final seal of Frenchness on the social dancing of Scotland. Her French forebears' and her own legacy was the development of basse dances, branles, and the like – couple dances which progressed round the room to the accompaniment of popular ballad tunes.

Outside the royal palaces, in the great houses, and among the ordinary people, the court dances were added to the regular repertoire of reels, ring dances and the last of the guild and mummers' dances.

In the English court in the second half of the 16th century, formal, Italian 'high' dances were intermingling with another form of social dancing in which couples took their places in long lines down the room, rather than round it. These dances involved a continuous progression down the dance so that the top couple could be replaced with each repetition of the dance. The English called this country dancing.

A visitor to the English court, Monsieur de Maisse, noted in 1597, that Elizabeth told him she took great pleasure in dancing and music and 'rebukes her Maids if they do not dance to her liking'.

And even as late as September 1602, a few months before her death, it was noted: 'We are here frolic at court, much dancing in the privy chamber of country dances before the Queen's majesty, who is exceedingly pleased withall.'

It was to this court, the English court, that Mary's son James was to come very soon as king of a united Scotland and England.

3

'FOR AS MANY AS WILL'

In the years which followed Mary's abdication, in 1567, in favour of her infant son James, Scotland was again at the mercy of factions and regents and ruled more and more by a Calvinist Kirk which grew in strength and power by the year.

Scotland had recently participated in a reformation that was the nearest Scotland ever got to total revolution, and it is surprising any kind of normal life proceeded in the years after 1560.

But there was not only life, but progress. Moves were afoot to establish, even in these troubled times, a school in each parish to offer an education to all. Scotland's five universities, St Andrews, Glasgow, Edinburgh and two in Aberdeen, were, in spite of the religious upheavals, producing men of international fame. It was an era, too, of building. The new middle class and the lairds provided themselves with town houses in Edinburgh's Royal Mile, as well as modernizing their country keeps.

Theologians and ministers of the new Protestant religion abounded, John Knox and, later, Andrew Melville being but the foremost of a considerable group of men, each commanding respect.

There were poets such as Montgomerie and Hume, Alexander Scott and the anonymous ballad writers of memorable works including *Sir Patrick Spens*, *The Twa Corbies*, *Lord Randal*.

There was also produced at this time the Scottish *Psalter*, the metric version of the Psalms of David which are still sung in Scottish churches. Undoubtedly they are better sung now than they were at first. The Reformed Kirk had been so anxious to remove anything that smacked of Popery that along with the kirk organs they had thrown out the musicians and the choirs. In subsequent despair at the sounds which emanated from congregations asked to do their own singing for the first time ever, the Kirk was forced to re-establish and to foster Sang Skuils. These were colleges of music attached to the churches, mostly associated with larger burghs, notably Aberdeen, to perform the new church music.

In time, congregations learned to sing and the Sang Skuils had the interesting side-effect on Scottish social history of producing successive generations of trained musicians and of making the learning of musical skills an honourable tradition which was encouraged in the young.

The early church had taken over pagan ceremonial and brought it under the church's wing, permitting dancing inside churches as well as in their environs. Naturally any such activity which survived was a prime target for the reformers.

The May Games were most ruthlessly disposed of – possibly because they had, over the years, become distinctly profane. Christmas celebrations, too, were stopped. Any Mass was anathema – and an end was put to the appointing of an Abbot of Unreason and a Lord of Bonaccord wherever these characters had ruled the festivities around Yule.

That the reformers did not succeed in killing off the old ways entirely is manifested every year in Scotland at Hallowe'en and at Hogmanay! But it is only within living memory that any widespread celebration of Christmas has taken place. Christmas Day, until the 1950s, was an ordinary working day for most Scots.

Sabbath, it was decided, was to be the only true holy day since it was the only day thus ordained by God. The reformers thereupon set about devising a Sabbath which has been described as 'designed as a foretaste of Hell, or as a source of revenue from fines imposed upon those who broke it'.

Hitherto, under the Roman Church, Sunday had been a day of recreation as well as of worship. Now there was to be positively no trading, no work and, above all, no entertainment. Folk in various parts of the country were fined for their 'insolence' in foot-racing and dancing on a Sunday. St Andrews Kirk Session, in 1574, appointed six persons to tour the town every Sunday and arrest any who transgressed kirk laws. All over the country the Kirk's appointees kept prying eyes on their neighbours with a marked zeal.

Another outrage against not only church law but also the law of the land came to the fore at this time. Witchcraft 'broke out' in Scotland in almost plague proportions. There was hardly a parish or a burgh without a witch fit to bring before the courts.

It has been suggested by modern social historians that this sudden manifestation of witchcraft – from those who were possibly dabbling in black arts to those parish simpletons and eccentrics who became inevitable scapegoats in a witch-hunt – was the direct result of the Kirk's attempts to smother every natural impulse under a cloak of respectability and godliness. The Scottish people had an innate love of laughter, gaiety, dancing and sports. The attempt to repress this natural behaviour gave rise to devastating guilt feelings in the more impressionable members of society and, in those who had perhaps indulged a little in the proscribed activities, guilt which produced breast-beating confessions of 'sins' – mostly undefined.

Public dancing, firmly held by the Kirk to be an unnatural activity, with all its evident 'lewdness' – kissing and the opportunity for the opposite sexes to touch each other – was, of course, a device of the devil.

One of the chief spokesmen against witchcraft, to the extent of writing a book on the subject, was the king himself. James was a shrewd and sensible man in many ways but his passion against witchcraft knew no sense.

Did he as a child hear that his mother had surely been bewitched by her lover and husband, James, Earl of Bothwell? Suspicions of witchcraft dogged both the Earl James and his successor Francis. Or was some attempt made to explain the king's physical deformities, his uneven gait, his over-large tongue, as evidence of some witch's curse put on his poor mother? Supposition – but there is nothing supposed about the manner in which witches, real and imagined, were pursued and persecuted in Scotland during and after his reign.

Witchcraft and public dancing were inextricably linked in the Kirk's eyes. And reports of witches dancing in rings are a feature of Scottish witchcraft trials.

But, witch-hunting apart, what of this young king who was to earn the title 'God's Silly Vassal' but who was also known as 'Shauchlin' Jamie', whose dancing master was paid extra for his extraordinary pains in attempting to teach the king to dance the social dances of the day?

Those ill-matched legs never made much of dancing in spite of the dancing master's efforts, nor was there any success in the encouragement to attain a little courtliness given to him by his distant relative, the Frenchman Esmé Stuart, whom he much admired for his manners and good looks. Stuart was created Duke of Lennox for his kindness and affection, but the king remained an ungainly youth, lacking in grace, 'uncouth in manner and disliking intensely and impatient with the trivialities of court life'.

When the time came for marriage, dynastic considerations came first. He was, after all, likely to be King of England one day. Therefore, a Protestant princess must be found, and was – in Denmark. Anne of Denmark has been variously described as tall, well-built, statuesque, charmingly girlish, and is universally considered to have been pleasant with nothing whatever behind her serene eyes.

She loved to dance and was particularly fond of the formal and vastly expensive court masques which had become the fashion in the courts of Europe. In order to please his new bride,

James ordered Scottish dancers to perform for her at their wedding celebrations in Edinburgh in 1590. The celebrations proved an expensive affair, the lavishness being excused by James who declared that it was justified because the King of Scots doesn't bring a bride home every day – for which Edinburgh's Town Treasurer must have been indeed thankful!

Among the accounts for the celebrations are found 'expenses dispensed upon the sword dance and hieland dances'. The sword dance mentioned is believed to have been a performance of the Perth Glovers' Dance, a trade guild dance with Morris, mummer and buffons trappings, last performed in Perth on a platform set up in the River Tay in the presence of James's son, Charles I, in 1633. There is an account of the performance given to Charles which would have been very similar to the one given to Anne and James forty years earlier.

The dancers' basic costume was of fawn cloth hung about with green and red trimmings. At the Edinburgh performance for James and Anne the dancers were furnished with white shoes, flower hats and bells. Small, round bells were very much a feature of the Glovers' costumes. A dress dating from the early 19th century and believed to be an accurate reproduction is preserved in the Perth Museum and Art Gallery. It is hung about lavishly with small bells on the ends of thongs of varying lengths. The bells were all tuned in such a way as to make a pleasant, harmonic accompaniment to the dance.

For Charles I, thirteen dancers performed on the river Tay, 'whereupon was ane flat stage of timber clad with birks. Whier upon thirteen of our brethren of this calling of glovers, with green caps, silver strings, reid ribbons, white shoes and bells about their legs, schearing rapers in their hands, and all other abulziment, danced our sword dance, with many different knots and allafallajessa and five being under the five above their shoulders, three of them dancing through their feet, drinking wine and breaking of glasses about them which, God be praised, was acted without hurt or skaith to any, which draws us to great charges amounting to the sum of 350 merks.' Thus ran the contemporary account of what must have been a dangerous and expensive ploy, a mixture of sword dance and acrobatics, with broken glass for an extra thrill. The royal reaction to either of these performances is not recorded.

At Anne and James's wedding celebrations it is not certain whether the Perth Glovers were the men referred to as Highlanders or if there was, in fact, another group of dancers from a more distant Highland place also in Edinburgh performing Highland dancing.

Certainly, the Perth Glovers' Dance with its stylized

movements might have been quite to the taste of Anne who was so fond of masques. She was also quite familiar with the social dancing of the day described carefully in Thoinot Arbeau's *Orchésographie* published just two years before, in 1588.

In Arbeau's book we are told that branles had developed regional characteristics and, as already mentioned, there is a detailed description of the Branle d'Ecosse. It has been noted by dance historians that the step for the Branle d'Ecosse is akin to the strathspey setting step of modern Scottish country dancing. One longs to find a similar 'Scottishness' in the tunes Arbeau gives for the dance, but must come to the conclusion that the Scottish quality of Arbeau's particular dance as performed in France was confined to the steps. However, from this it can be deduced that there must have been at that time steps and movements which were recognized as characteristically Scottish. And if this branle were danced in Scotland, then the music provided there would have all the essential Scottishness required!

In any event, dancing at the Scottish court would, by 1590, have been a little less French in style and a little more 'native'. Galliards, though, remained a favourite dance, perhaps because they had a little of the 'reeland' about them – partners dancing not so much together as side by side and towards each other, with the chance to show off steps a little.

Twenty years had passed since the French influence began to wane, and, in face of France's threats to restore a Catholic monarchy to Scotland, the Scots had at last turned their eyes to England – as a friend. Despite Elizabeth's unwillingness to name him as her successor, it was unlikely that there could be any other valid claimant on her death than James VI of Scotland.

One suspects Queen Anne could not wait to get to England when her husband was finally sent for in 1603. England was a wealthier realm by far than Scotland and there, surely, she would be allowed to command the finest musicians, painters, designers, actors and dancers to present her beloved masques with all their classical poetry, stylized dancing and wondrous stage effects.

Not everyone shared her enthusiasm for the road south. James's Scottish retainers and court knew they were considered by their English counterparts to be very much the shabby, poor relations. But they travelled proud. As lawyer Thomas Craig wrote: 'We do not mind our neighbours sneering at our lack of wealth. For wealth and material resources are not everything, otherwise we should long ago have lost our liberty and fallen under the domination of the English.'

As the Scottish court processed down the high road to England, they left behind them a country which was inevitably socially bereft by their departure. The town of Edinburgh would no longer be the headquarters of a royal court, and, just as the causeways would no longer resound to skirmishes between rival earls and lords, the palace at the end of the street would no longer serve as the focus of social attention, pointing the fashion in clothes, in manners, in dancing.

It was almost eighty years before Holyrood became a royal residence once more – and then for only two years. In the interim, much happened to the dance.

Once arrived in London, James's queen, Anne, was allowed to give her taste for masques full rein and now it became the turn of London Treasurers to complain about the crippling expense of it all. The queen constantly overspent on these entertainments, and the king indulged her. Court balls were lavish affairs in which couple dances, such as corantos performed in the leaping English manner, were alternated with the country dances which had become so popular by the end of Elizabeth's reign.

Although the present writer has been unable to find any extant account, it is hard to believe that the Scottish court did not continue to enjoy their own forms of dancing at the English court. And it is at this point in dance history that many tunes popular for dancing to in Scotland found their way, along with their titles, into the English country-dance repertoire. If 'Scottish' was a synonym for rustic or crude or peasantlike at the English court, then it is likely that Scottish dance modes and tunes were adopted at first to bolster the rusticity of country dances – to make them seem even more country at court. It is good to think of the newly prestigious Scotsmen in the Palace of Whitehall swinging into a reel as light relief from some tedious, elaborate masque. It certainly would have been entirely in the *Scottish* character to have done so.

Scottish influence on English country dancing in the first half of the 17th century was considerable, and remained so in the following centuries when the country dance was in its heyday, and the early Scottish influence on country dancing is manifest as the evidence of tunes and titles published in the first English country-dance instruction books shows.

Life in Scotland, without its own court, went on. Rule by a distant king who paid only one further visit in his lifetime, in 1617 for a brief twelve weeks, created a succession of internal problems. Parliament and the Presbyterian Kirk were in a constant state of quarrel.

The history of the 17th century brings forward names like Cromwell, the Covenanters, Killiecrankie, Montrose, Glencoe, the Darien Scheme. Nothing much there to set the feet tapping. But there were other aspects of Scottish life, which were forming the background for the eventual popularity of social dancing.

In the Stuart years, from 1603 to 1714, the middle class continued to grow in Scotland. Traders and merchants, purveyors and suppliers, all eagerly took advantage of the new and relatively stable economic climate to thrive as never before. With Holyrood no longer the focal point of the city of Edinburgh, these merchants, traders and lesser nobility crammed into the newly built heights of the Netherbow in the Royal Mile. Tall eight and ten storey tenements teemed, and the whole of life was enjoyed in the daily passing-show.

One Englishman wrote: 'This street, which may indeed deserve to dominate the whole city, is always thronged with people, it being the market place, and is the only place where the gentlemen and merchants meet and walk, wherein they may walk dry underfoot . . .'

Overhead was a different matter. The merchants and gentlemen would have had to take great care to duck the contents of the refuse pails jettisoned from upper windows to the accompaniment of the cry 'Gardyloo'.

In an intimate society such as Edinburgh's was, there existed a rough and ready all-Jock-Tamson's-bairns democracy. What the upper classes did, the middle classes imitated, to be copied, or parodied, by the common folk – all of them likely to live in the same building, stacking their ordure together at the same front entrance. In no other city in the country did all the classes live so cheek-by-jowl and this proximity made for a singular richness and variety of life as well as a strong interdependence. The grandest lady in Edinburgh was as likely as the meanest to wrap her head and shoulders in a plaid shawl to go on some errand; the meanest lady's shawl would, at times, have been as clean as M'lady's!

The young city of Glasgow at this time was growing up in quite a different manner which would in its time affect the social life of that city. In Glasgow the classes early lived apart – and grew apart.

The Kirk, in the midst of internal turmoils and in revolt against Episcopacy, still eagerly sought the power to control the lives of the people. Excess of any kind was utterly condemned (with the apparent exception of excess within the Kirk itself, such as when gallons of fine wine and dozens of loaves of good bread were consumed as part of the sacrament of Holy

Communion). Excess was deemed to include having too many guests at a baptism or a funeral, and the time-honoured Scottish custom of the penny wedding came under the constant surveillance and attempted stricture of the Kirk.

Popular both in the burghs and in the countryside a penny wedding was an affair which could attract hundreds of roistering guests who celebrated for days on end. When the word went out that such a wedding was to take place, neighbours, friends and casual acquaintances for miles around would assemble on the appointed day, each bearing gifts of food or drink to furnish the feast, or some money to fee the musicians.

Penny weddings were, naturally, noisy affairs. They were held in ale-houses and barns, or out of doors if the weather was fine. The noise didn't bother the neighbours since they were all present, but it did trouble the Kirk. A lot of noise was a sure indication of excess!

Attempts were made soon after 1560 to control penny weddings and in the following century the attempts became more serious and the punishments for contravention of kirk laws more severe. A particular target of the Kirk were the pipers, fiddlers and balladeers who were an essential part of the proceedings and, it was surmised, the cause of all the din. The idea was to discourage them and thus discourage the revelry.

When that failed and the singing, the speechmaking, the toasts and the dancing went on apace, the control of numbers was attempted. To begin with, a restriction to forty guests, twenty for the bride and twenty for the groom, was tried. And if this number was exceeded, or if there was any other cause for complaint against the party, a sum of money deposited with the parish clerk as warranty of good behaviour was forfeited.

Pipers who played both before and after the meal in order to encourage the noise of singing and dancing were brought before kirk sessions for punishment. But large, noisy penny weddings continued. After all, what was to prevent three or more couples marrying on the same day with all their sets of forty guests coming together for the fray?

Ritual reels called Bridal Reels were for many hundreds of years part of Scottish wedding celebrations and Bridal Reels continued into this century in the Northern Isles and in remoter mainland places. The Bridal Reel was normally a foursome performed by the bride, the groom, the best man and the bridesmaid – or else a sixsome in which the four were joined by another older couple as symbols of a happy marriage, perhaps.

Other wedding rituals involved customs and rites which, with their evident fertility symbolism, went back to pagan days.

The Kirk, though, did not succeed in stopping these rituals, nor in stopping penny weddings, nor, indeed, in reforming all of Scotland.

In large areas from Aberdeenshire westwards and north, the lords and lesser lairds had quietly adhered to the Roman Church or become Episcopalians during the early years of the 17th century. It was in these areas that the old ways proceeded unhindered by the Kirk's threats and not much troubled by its censure and parish punishment. It was there that the Presbyterians might girn all they liked – but if the laird said 'On with the dance!' then on it went, pipers, fiddlers and all.

Meantime, at the English court, longways country dancing had developed in style and popularity and it was this form of social dancing which was, by the end of the 17th century, to become the 'Darling and favourite Diversion of all ranks of people'.

Dancing longways – two lines of dancers, men on one side and women on the other, facing each other down the length of a room – was known in 15th-century Italy but we cannot be sure of when it found its way to this country. As has been noted, a longways dance is listed in *The Complaynt of Scotland* of 1549. And by the end of the 16th century these dances were much favoured by Queen Elizabeth's court where their charm must have lain in their simple qualities which would provide an antidote to overdoses of the acrobatic couple dancing which Elizabeth favoured. At any event, by the time country dances gained popularity with Elizabeth, she was a little too old to go flying round her partner's head at La Volta and her love of dancing would have attracted her to the simpler, more floor-bound country dancing.

The popularity of longways country dancing outside the court is testified to by references to specific country dances in works such as Rycharde's *Misogonus* which first appeared around 1560.

'Can you dance country dances?' asks a character, to receive as reply a list of dances which included The Shaking of the Sheets, Putney Ferry and Heartsease. Used thus in a play for public performance, the author would naturally have chosen titles familiar to his audience which would have comprised common folk as well as courtiers.

The Shaking of the Sheets was also known as The Dede Dance, which provides a link with the Deid Dance of *The Complaynt of Scotland*, eleven years earlier. That they were indeed popular dances is further indicated by the length of time they remained popular – for the same dances turn up in the manuals of dancing published by John Playford a hundred years later.

Much energy has been expended on claiming country dances as either Scottish or English in origin. The clues are usually the tunes since these dances from the outset have taken their titles from the tunes to which they were danced. It is often possible to say such and such a tune was Scottish in origin, and another was English and yet another Irish. But there seems little point in pursuing the 'who was first' line of investigation, as there was always constant traffic of tunes between the countries of the British Isles. And it is plain that longways country dancing was known both in England and Scotland long before the first dance manuals were published in England.

The differences which emerged between the native Scottish and the English style of dancing country dances were the Scots' mode of strong rhythmic music and the dance steps developed and taught by succeeding generations of Scottish dancing masters. In Scotland dancing masters took the native steps and polished them, probably encouraging their use in the ballroom. In England there seems to have been comparatively little intricate footwork to develop so that the concentration of the masters was focused on schooling their charges in the correct procedures of the dance, elegant running steps and gracious manners.

When John Playford published the first edition of *The English Dancing Master*, in 1650, the movements of the dance and the musical phrasing of the movements were clearly set out, but no actual steps were described, only figures.

Dances are prefaced by such general instructions as 'Longways for six' or 'Longways for as many as will'. He uses words and phrases which give a first-class notion of how a dance progressed: 'First man set to his owne [partner], the second man salute his owne and turn her. First man and last woman change places. Lead up. Sides all. Armes all.' Excellent descriptions of the movement of everything but the feet which are mentioned only in his Table explaining the Characters which are set down in the Dances. 'A double is four steps forward or back, closing both feet. A single is two steps, closing both feet.'

All of which makes one wonder if the positioning of the feet ever had much importance in the English form of country dancing – and today it is performed in a sort of ambling skip with none of the balletic footwork which marks its Scottish counterpart.

Playford's *The English Dancing Master*, called simply *The Dancing Master* in its later editions, is a significant landmark in the story of country dancing, for it was the first attempt to publish a large selection of tunes and the dances they accompanied.

The English Dancing Master was not originally addressed to the general public but it became a huge commercial success. In his lifetime, Playford became accustomed to commercial success. He produced many very fine editions and collections of contemporary music, his music shop was both a fashionable and practical rendezvous for amateur and professional musicians alike. By dedicating his book to the Gentlemen of the Inns of Court he was allying himself to an influential group known and respected as dancers. They had, on several occasions, provided elegant masques for royal audiences and were renowned for the quality of their dancing.

The very title, The English Dancing Master, used for the first edition was bound to catch the public eye. Twelve years or so before the appearance of the book there had been presented in London a play called The Varietie in which a highly comic character called Monsieur Galliard taught dancing. So memorable was this character, and so popular with audiences, that the play was subsequently retitled The French Dancing Master. Twenty years later, in 1662, The French Dancing Master was still playing to delighted audiences.

John Playford made no secret of his active dislike of French dancing, of French dancing masters and of the contemporary fashion for employing French musicians, and probably hit on the title for his collection of dances as a riposte. Whatever his reasons, the book was an instant success and it, and his other publications brought him as printer and publisher royal recognition in his lifetime. On his death in 1686, Purcell composed the Elegy upon my friend Mr. John Playford.

The popularity of the book is evidence enough of the popularity of country dancing at that time. The Dancing Master ran to eighteen editions in all and was produced after John's death by his son Henry and then later by one John Young. The last edition appeared in 1725 by which time the market was well and truly awash with books of country dances.

In 1636, in the reign of Charles I, Charles Butler, writing in The Principles of Music, says that ballads are 'sett unto sundry pleasant and delightful tunes by cunning and witty composers with country dances fitted unto them'. An aspect of dancing which would have appealed to the very musical King Charles and his French queen, Henrietta Maria.

Charles loved country dancing and it was a favourite part of revels at court. We have an eye-witness account of how Charles 'did lead the measures with the French Ambassador's wife, the measures, branles, corantos and galliards being ended, the masquers with the ladies did dance two Country Dances, the Soldiers March and Halfe Hanniken'.

Always, country dancing seems to have had a place as welcome relief from the formal couple dances and the masques. And the dance music was a source of delight in its lightness and gaiety.

Queen Henrietta Maria, who had a remarkably fine singing voice and who was an accomplished performer of the classical dance movements of the formal masques, may have been, at the first, taken aback by country dancing. Certainly some of her French retainers reporting home expressed astonishment at the dancing at court, which involved a mixing of rank practically unheard of in French court circles.

Not everyone in England, however, approved of the style of dancing at court. In John Selden's *Table Talk* there appears this account of the dancing of the day:

'The Court of England is much altered. At a Solemn dancing, first you have the grave measures, then the corantos and the galliards, and all this is kept up with ceremony, at length they fall to trenchmore, and so to the cushion dance, lord and groom, lady and kitchen maid, no distinction: so in our Court. In Queen Elizabeth's time, gravity and state were kept up. In King James time things were pretty well. But in King Charles time there has been nothing but trenchmore and the cushion dance, Omnium gatherum, tolly polly, hoyte come toyte.'

John Selden was an eminent lawyer of his day and a very active anti-Royalist before and during the Civil War, thus he was hardly likely to approve of anything which happened in Charles's court and, despite his account, it would be going altogether too far to suggest that country dancing at court was classless. When the lines of dancers took their places the top couples were of the highest rank, the last couples of the lowest. But, as far as the French were concerned, the fact that the top couple didn't always stay at the head of the dance but might be replaced as the dance proceeded by the second, third, fourth couple and so on, was revolutionary.

That this form of dancing was enjoyed by every stratum of society must have been its salvation during the Puritan regime of Oliver Cromwell. Even good Puritans like John Bunyan found it difficult to accept that there was any harm in country dancing.

And it is a curious fact that *The English Dancing Master* appeared in 1650 – only a few months after the execution of Charles I and the establishment of the Commonwealth under Lord Protector Cromwell.

But mixed dancing, in Scotland as well as in England, was condemned by the Puritans as profane. The promiscuity of country dancing with couples not only giving hands but changing partners, not to mention the utter profanity of the kisses still, on occasion, used to begin and end a dance – all were abhorrent to the stricter Puritans. With the zeal of the newly powerful, they closed down places of public entertainment and sought to control public celebrations. But they could do little to control what went on in the privacy of homes and country dancing continued behind closed doors.

Playford's dedication of *The English Dancing Master* to 'the Gentlemen of the Inns of Court, whose sweet and ayry Activity has crowned their Grand solemnities with admiration to all spectators' may be an indication that the lawyers sometimes danced country dances without female partners. Certainly they would have danced with ladies at the end of their masques but, since country dances were often actually introduced into the masques themselves, particularly when a rustic scene was being set, the Gentlemen of the Inns may have practised new country dances without ladies. At about this time, in order to side-step Puritan and Presbyterian objections to promiscuous dancing, men did dance with men and women with women. And in the Scottish regiments of the British Army, formed then and in succeeding centuries, soldiers were, and still are, taught reels and country dances to be performed by men only.

In England Puritan prohibitions were of short duration. By 1657 the French Ambassador to Cromwell's 'court' was reporting that dances, fêtes and like entertainments were returning and, in the same year, at the marriage of Cromwell's daughter, Frances, there was 'mixt' dancing into the early hours of the morning, to the accompaniment of an orchestra of forty-eight violins and fifty trumpets.

Compared to the alternative 'French' dances, as the formal couple dances were sometimes called, the essential sociability of country dancing is nowhere better expressed than in *The Mysteries of Love and Elegance*, a play by Edward Philips, a nephew of the poet Milton. 'Will you be pleased,' asks a character, 'to dance a Country Dance or two, for 'tis that which makes you truly sociable – being like the chorus of a song where all parts sing together.'

With the Restoration of Charles II, in 1660, there was a steady revival of dancing and revelry. Court balls were grand, becoming lavish, and conducted with a mixture of formality and informality.

It was in the second half of the century, too, that country dancing from the British Isles began to become popular on the Continent, particularly at the French court where they may first have been seen danced by Charles II's exiled courtiers during Cromwell's years, and where they were called *Contre Danses* –

contre being quite simply a corruption of the English word 'country' and having nothing whatever to do with *contre* meaning against or opposite.

In Europe at this time and, again, particularly in France, dancing was considered an essential part of a young gentleman's education. King Louis XIV of France took a daily dancing lesson for twenty years from his Dance Master Beauchamp who is believed to have created the minuet.

In the training of a young man about court, dancing was in the same league as horsemanship, weapon-training and knowing how to conduct oneself. Monsieur de Muralt, a Swiss observer of the British scene in the second half of the 17th century, declared he knew no other nobility which neglected so much horsemanship, weaponry and the like as did the British. However, he went on to admire the abandon with which they threw themselves into the country dance. Nowhere else in Europe did country dancing achieve the same gaiety and cross-class quality that it did in Britain.

M. de Muralt remarked on this crossing of class boundaries in country dancing, 'The ordinary people take the same pleasure [in dancing] as do the nobles, merchants and clergy.' He also noticed that in all facets of British life, nobles and ordinary folk mixed together. They could be seen at the same venues, the same pleasure resorts and public gardens – 'even at their dances, which require many people taking part, I have been told that in the country when the number isn't great enough, they think nothing of getting their servants to make up the number'.

The Abbé Prevost, another visitor to these shores, watched the nobility dance and wrote in his *Mémoires*: 'Ordinarily, they begin their balls with minuets' – introduced to Charles II's court in the 1660s from France – 'and then come the country dances. They join up to form two lines, fifteen or twenty men with as many women; it is possible to have an even greater number dancing if the room is large enough; and without the least confusion, they turn, jump, cross over in a thousand ways. The tunes have a vivacity which moves the spirit. The women are the most intrepid dancers I have seen in all my life. They never seem to tire, even when in a state of constant movement for four or five hours on end.'

At court, then, after the formal dancing – during which the king and queen might dance together or with partners of very high rank, the others assembled choosing partners of equal rank – the royal pecking order seems to have been cast aside for the country dances. Country dances were highly sociable and it was this very quality which endeared them to people at every level of British society.

Samuel Pepys, in his famous diary, gives this description of a court ball in 1662:

'By and by comes the King [Charles II] and Queen. The Duke and Duchess [of York], and all the great ones; and after seating themselves the King takes out the Duchess of York, and the Duke the Duchess of Buckingham; the Duke of Monmouth my Lady Castlemaine; and so other lords, other ladies; and they danced the Bransle. After that, the King led a lady in a single Coranto; and then the rest of the Lords, one after another, other ladies; very noble it was and a great pleasure to see. Then to country dances; the King leading the first, which he called for; which was, says he "Cuckolds all awry" the old dance of England.'

At the French court at that time the king and queen together, or one or other with a suitable partner, would perform the opening dance while everyone watched. Only after this would the king or the queen, or both, choose another partner and the guests would then be partnered by those of equal rank. The order of rank in the dance was rigidly and invariably adhered to.

The Comte de Grammont who was a French visitor at the court of Charles II and an eager reporter of all he saw, wrote that the English were not good at the slow stately court dances 'in spite of there being some of the best dancers in the world amongst them'. At balls, as soon as possible, 'they left the French [court dances] and went to the country dances'.

It seems, from de Grammont, that French observers regarded country dances at that time as an inferior sort of dancing which did not require much expertise – just enthusiasm.

De Grammont left one delightful cameo of a typical English gentleman – the Hon. John Russell, ageing bachelor third son of the Earl of Bedford, and country dance enthusiast *sans pareil*.

'Russell was one of the most furious dancers in all England, I mean for country dances; he had a collection of two or three hundred in print, all of which he danced at sight; and to prove that he was not an old man, he sometimes danced until he was almost exhausted; his mode of dancing was like that of his clothes, for they both had been out of fashion full twenty years.'

From these remarks it seems that there were, even to a foreign observer, perceptible changes occurring in the style of country dancing. Were these changes in the steps, or the movements, or were.they in the approach to and the manner of the dance?

One suspects the last would have been the answer. The dances would have undergone considerable change as they lost their rustic rumbustiousness and the Hon. John's 'fury' in the dance would now be out of fashion. Country dancing had become gradually more sophisticated and refined through use at court. In addition, there were the activities of dancing masters throughout the country who were already cashing in on the popularity of country dancing as a proper pastime for the middle classes.

Very soon, due in considerable measure to the activities of these men, there was general recognition of dancing as an essential part of a young person's upbringing. Young English and Scottish noblemen and the sons of the upper middle class sought a 'finishing' education in Europe where they hoped to be trained in the gentlemanly arts which had long included dancing. Those who could not afford to travel, learned their skills from instructors who set up salons and schools throughout Britain.

Instrumental music, too, was considered an essential part of a proper education and there exist today several important collections of instrumental and vocal music made by young Scotsmen of the time.

Therefore, when James, Duke of York, Charles II's brother, arrived with his retainers and his Duchess to take up residence at Holyrood in 1680, he came to a country where the nobility and the middle class, at least, were *au fait* with the cultural requirements of polite society.

The minuet was, by this time, all the rage. The corantos, branles and galliards had almost vanished in face of the elegance and charm of the minuet which was to be the favourite couple dance for a hundred and fifty years until the arrival of the waltz at the end of the next century.

Dancing masters from Britain hastened to France – or at least said they did in their advertisements – to learn the correct manner of the minuet. French dancing masters hurried here – or at least said they did in their advertisements – to learn new country dances.

Meanwhile, in Edinburgh's Royal Mile, everyone – from the wigmaker's wife, to the kitchen maids, to the lawyers' ladies – was strenuously copying the new 'betters' in the newly remodelled Holyrood Palace. The Duke and Duchess were in residence there for two years, and Scotland's social life received a distinct fillip during that time.

The Duke succeeded his brother Charles II as King James VII and II, in 1685, and presided over a court which differed considerably from that of the late, lascivious and much lamented Merry Monarch. Dancing, however, continued to be the chief amusement.

The French dancing master, André Lorin, who presented his

Livre de Contredanse to King Louis XIV around 1686, has much to say about country dancing in Britain. De Grammont had reported that everyone inside and outside court circles enjoyed country dancing and Lorin reinforced this by reporting that in the course of his researches he had travelled round the country in order to see how the mode of dancing had varied from place to place.

'I have seen them dance not only at court and at town assemblies, but again at schools' [dance schools, that is], 'at masquerades' [public dances where the participants were masked], 'at musicales' [public dances where one danced to the accompaniment of a variety of instruments], 'and in the open air.'

Infuriatingly, Monsieur Lorin, having told us where he watched dancing, doesn't go on to record the differences he observed from place to place. For the benefit of his royal reader he reports simply on the dancing at the court of James VII and II – but with an eye for detail and a professional interest and knowledge which makes his account both valuable and interesting.

He observes that, in spite of the overriding popularity of the country dances – dances longways for as many as wished to take part – there was another kind of country dancing which was also performed quite often in 'round the room' formation with positions and a mixture of figures 'not seen in the others'.

Can it be that James and his court had picked up some steps and dances during their Scottish 'exile'? Certainly the dances must have been significantly different for Lorin to comment on them.

He also recounts how James's court enjoyed two kinds of ball. There was the extremely formal ball for which everyone dressed sumptuously and which took place in a room 'previously set aside and specifically decorated for dancing' – a ballroom, in fact. The other kind, much less formal, took place in the king's private apartments. At these dances the court enjoyed country dances in a very carefree manner, not even bothering to dress up for the occasion. That must have startled Louis whose very rising from bed, attended by ritual and formality, was a matter of public spectacle.

The dance in King James's private apartments proceeded under the direction of their Majesties who placed their guests in a column of couples, 'in the order they had prescribed' and led them into a room cleared for dancing. There everyone took their places in two lines facing the top of the room where the king was, the men on the left of the file with their ladies on their right.

The first couple ordered the tune for the country dance of their choice and then everyone made a bow and curtsey to the king, made a quarter turn to face each other, and the dance began. Every dancer knew when to move up and down the dance, when to turn together, make room for the leading dancers to pass, and so on. Successive heying (making the figure eight, turning, passing, setting) presented a picture of perpetual motion to the observer, and placed the top couple back in their original position at the head of the dance. After a bow and curtsey to each other, they then walked to the foot of the dance. Couple number two became top couple and called for the country dance of their choice, and the whole thing began again with everyone in motion.

In this way a large number and variety of dances were danced in an evening. A very popular dance could be called for several times, and there is no evidence that the modern method of progression, where each couple in turn becomes top couple *while a single dance is repeated several times*, was commonly employed.

At functions more public than parties in the royal apartments, this method, too, helped to prevent any arguments about who chose the dance. It was the choice of the couple at the top of the set, those further down the line must wait their turn. And there was a nice touch of gallantry in that no matter from which level of society the couples came, the man chose the woman with whom he wished to dance but left the choice of the dance to her when they reached the top of the set.

According to Lorin, in this fashion it was possible to perform upwards of fifty different country dances in an evening at a single ball. He presented fifty-seven dances in his manuscript which included, he said, dances specially written by an English dancing master for certain people at the French court.

Such was the popularity of country dancing that, despite dynastic troubles and internal wars in both Scotland and England, dancing never flagged as the most popular pastime of all. There always seemed to be a time and a place for dancing.

When King James abdicated, in 1689, he was succeeded by William III and his wife Mary II, who ruled the country jointly. Mary, true Stuart that she was, was passionately fond of dancing and its continuity as a court pleasure was assured. So much, indeed, did Mary prefer country dancing and its music to any other form of entertainment that she is said once to have sent for the composer Purcell, making him sit through repeated performances of the old ballad Cold and Raw which was a popular country dance tune of the time. *That*, she informed the foremost English composer of his day, was what *she* called a good tune!

It had been a century of good tunes and of great changes in styles of dancing. There had been the banning of the May Games and the Yuletide revelries with Kirk and State in turn trying hard to control the occasions on which the people danced. The Perth Glovers had danced their ancient trade guild dance for the last recorded time. The figures, the setting and turning of the old reels had found their way into the country dances enjoyed at private parties, public balls and at court. Above all, the study of dancing had, in spite of the strictures of a disapproving Kirk, become part of a polite education – and in Scotland there were determined efforts being made to bring an education of sorts to everyone.

Country dancing had, from being an energetic 'rustic' amusement for the British, developed into a mode of dancing fit for the royal courts of Europe.

4
THE DARLING DIVERSION

The second half of the 18th century was truly Scotland's Golden Age when this small, sparsely populated, remote northland came to the forefront in philosophy, medicine, economics, invention.

Yet, the opening of the century found Scotland in economic tatters with the failure of the Darien Scheme – that ill-devised attempt at colonization on the Isthmus of Panama – a bitter memory, and the people divided over the 1707 Union with the Westminster Parliament.

This was not the climate in which one would expect much flourishing of the arts or social life. For thirty years and more after the Union, Scotland's economic life slowly recovered but, if English influence on material life was slow to make its mark, the effect on the social scene was quite another matter.

At the opening of the century, Scotland's nobility and gentry, in their ancient fortified country castles, or in their crammed Edinburgh tenements were a gregarious, talented and singularly unaffected crowd who loved to meet, to exchange gossip, to drink together, to listen to music and be otherwise entertained. Yet, the architecture of Edinburgh, although it made for couthiness and close acquaintance, hardly provided an appropriate setting for the appreciation of the finer things in life!

Nevertheless, at the turn of the century the arts in Edinburgh flourished – good music in particular, and performances of contemporary orchestral music were given regularly by an ensemble of thirty players, eleven of whom were professional music teachers in the town. An appreciation of music and attendance at concerts was part of Edinburgh life, and learning a variety of instruments was considered an essential part of a young lady or gentleman's education.

It was to a gifted, cultured group, then, in spite of the setting in which they found themselves, that news came of the entertainment which was the current rage of English high society when it ventured to the watering place of Bath.

Bath had, since the days of the Romans, been famous for its hot springs round which had grown a little town. To Bath, down the centuries, had come generations of invalids and sightseers to visit the baths and otherwise amuse themselves. But despite the patronage of Catherine of Braganza, Charles II's queen, by the beginning of the 18th century the spa was out of fashion and had fallen into a state of filth, neglect and disrepute.

Then, in 1703, it was visited by Queen Anne who took the waters doubtless in search of some bodily comfort. (Poor Anne had to endure in her life a wearisome succession of pregnancies and stillbirths. Although she gave birth seventeen times, none of her children lived through babyhood.) And Bath, having received renewed royal approval, thereafter became a fashionable resort for the English rich whose chief work was filling their days. By 1705, five of those hours were being whiled away delightfully for them by a magnificently organized Public Dance Assembly – brainchild of Richard 'Beau' Nash.

There was a man with a splendid eye to the main chance. He deserves, indeed, to be made the patron saint of impressarios. So great was his influence on his adopted city that he, rather than Queen Anne, is still credited almost entirely with its revival as a fashionable centre!

What he did in establishing Public Assemblies was not entirely new – there had been other Public Assemblies, places where people paid for the pleasure of seeing and being seen dancing. The factors which made Nash's Assemblies the model to which society held the glass for many years, were the manner in which he conducted them and the rules which he laid down to ensure that all would be as smooth-running as possible.

In the succeeding decades there would be many imitators of Nash, the finest being the Scotsman MacCall who, sixty years later, transposed his name to Almack and subsequently ran the most fashionable Assembly rooms in London.

In a Nash Assembly, as in most of its successors – public, charitable or private – the conduct of the dancing was as carefully regulated as the membership. At Bath the programme began at six p.m. with minuets until eight p.m. Then from eight p.m. there was country dancing, with a break at nine p.m. for refreshment, through to the stroke of eleven when Nash would imperiously raise his hand to stop the music.

An early Edinburgh attempt at entertainment in the Assembly style is thought to have been connected with a fashionable club for men known as the Horn Order, founded in 1705. In the custom of the English clubs of the time, membership was all-male with women admitted only by invitation to certain events such as masked balls regarded as rather dubious affairs. Such activities, even under the auspices of the nobility, were hardly considered suitable for young ladies.

Around 1710 a form of private Assembly, which may have had its origins in the Horn Club, was begun in Edinburgh's West Bow. This was a street which led from the Grassmarket to the Lawnmarket in the Royal Mile, and of which only traces remain. Since, at the West Bow Assembly, there was gambling and drinking as well as dancing, this too was hardly the kind of place the Scottish gentry would wish to take their wives and daughters if they didn't want to be thought flying in the face of the Kirk altogether. In the moral and religious climate of the times, the censure of the Kirk was still something to be avoided.

And it must not be assumed that public dancing had found universal favour in England, where, according to the Scots, morality was notoriously more lax! A letter appearing in an issue of the *Spectator* in 1711, even if it is written tongue-in-cheek, reflects a prevalent attitude towards the vogue for dancing in public.

'My eldest daughter, a girl of sixteen, has for some time been under the tuition of Monsieur Rigadoon, a Dancing-Master in the City; and I was prevailed upon by her and her mother to go last night to one of his balls . . . I was amazed to see my girl handled by, and handling young fellows with so much familiarity; and I could not have thought it had been in the child. They very often made use of a most impudent and lascivious step called "setting", which I know not how to describe to you, but by telling you that 'tis the very reverse of "Back to Back". At last an impudent young dog bid the fiddlers to play a dance called Mol Pately, and after having made two or three capers, ran to his partner, locked his arms in hers, and whisked her round cleverly above ground in such manner, that I, who sat upon one of the lowest benches, saw further above her shoe than I think fit to acquaint you with.'

The reply to this would have done little to soothe the over-anxious and the literal-minded!

'I must confess I am afraid that my correspondent had too much reason to be a little out of humour at the treatment of his daughter, but I conclude he might have been much more so had he seen one of those kissing dances in which, Will Honeycomb assures me, they are obliged to dwell almost a minute on the fair one's lips, or they will be too quick for the music and dance quite out of time . . .'

In more serious vein, about this time, the exercise of country dancing *was* finding favour with good teachers of dancing who, like one Weaver, also writing in 1711, said: 'This dancing is a moderate and healthful exercise, a pleasant and innocent amusement, if modestly used, and performed at convenient times and by a suitable company.'

It was uncertainty of finding that 'suitable company' which led to the decline of Edinburgh's West Bow Assembly and the setting up, in 1723, of a new and well-regulated Assembly in the High Street. This new Assembly was organized much more in the order of Nash's Bath Assemblies. Admission was strictly controlled, but if a body had the right pedigree and the price of a ticket, then he was in.

The high fashion of Bath was, thereupon, set down in the High Street of Edinburgh which seems a little like setting a bunch of roses on a midden. But the High Street – and the new Assembly at the back of Patrick Steil's Close between St Giles' and the Tron Kirk – was the middenhead the Scottish gentry were used to, and they flocked to the Assembly.

The evenings' entertainments were organized by Lady Directresses, ladies of rank and quality and tremendous respectability. The original directresses were the Countess of Panmure and the Ladies Newhall, North Berwick, Orbistoun and Drumelzier and the names of the last two are to be found engraved on the surviving Directress' Badge of Office which is in the Scottish Museum of Antiquities. The badge is a medallion of silver which has engraved on one side, 'Edinburgh Assembly Anno Dom 1724. Ladies Drumelzier and Orbistoun'. And on the other side is an engraving of a lame beggar and the inscription, 'Nothing Availeth Without Charity'.

Charity – *that* was the magic word that softened the face of the Kirk towards the Assemblies and allowed mothers to let their daughters be seen dancing in public. In the many years of their existence, the various Edinburgh Assemblies gave most generously to charity and the Kirk simply could not gainsay these Christian acts of giving, even if it reserved the right to continue to preach against the promiscuous nature of the source of such generosity.

The portioning out of the Assembly profits was mainly at the discretion of these Lady Directresses who also had much of the responsibility for the hiring and running of the Assembly Rooms as well as acting as chaperones extraordinary. They had a rota for attendance at balls and their word was law. It was they who commanded the dancers, who placed the couples appropriately in their sets and who kept a watchful eye out for any interloper. Balls were held every Thursday from four in the afternoon until Nash's finishing hour of eleven. Refreshments in the form of tea, coffee, chocolate, with biscuits, were charged for over and above the price of half a crown (12½ pence) for the admission ticket. The catering was deputed to managers or, in the case of the Edinburgh Assemblies for many years, to manageresses, the Misses Robertson by name.

But no matter how well regulated and run, in those early years the Assembly was not totally accepted. In a pamphlet of the time entitled *A Letter from a gentleman in the country to his friend in the City, with an Answer thereto, concerning the New Assembly*, the writer is principally perturbed by the effects dancing is purported to have on the manliness of youth.

'I happened the other day to meet with a Gentleman who had been lately in town, and among other things, I presumed to enquire his thoughts of this new Assembly; he was pleased to tell me that the people in town were as widely different in their opinions about it as we are in the country; some approving, others disapproving of it, but that for his part, he believed it would prove a Machine of Luxury to soften and effeminate the minds of our young nobility and gentry, and that in some measure it had already this effect that they, instead of employing themselves in the useful arts and sciences that might some time render them capable to serve themselves, their friends and their country, now made it their greatest care who should be best equipped and dressed for the Assembly night and to strain their fancies to invent some agreeable Love Tattle to tell the Belle Creatures whom they shall happen most to admire in the meeting.'

Despite the doubts, the Assembly proceeded and was widely copied throughout Scotland. By the 1740s Glasgow had acquired for itself a teacher of dancing and a dance Assembly. Aberdeen and Dundee also had Assemblies, the former city with its strong musical and educational tradition had been holding public balls since before 1695, as it is on record that that year the Council forbade Mr Batham, their official Town Dancing Master, from 'having Publick Balls of dancing in this place'.

Public balls in Aberdeen in that era had frequently been the source of trouble because of drinking and rowdiness, but in later years the city had as douce an Assembly as any of its counterparts and 'country dances were kept up with great spirit to the lively Scotch tunes, and formed a most agreeable amusement, free from ceremony, every one on terms of intimacy'.

Since, at all Assemblies, the best part of the evening was given over to country dances, it may be assumed that in the first half of the 18th century they took on a considerable patina of gentility.

Kellom Tomlinson wrote in the preface to his *Art of Dancing* printed in 1735, 'country dancing is become, as it were, the Darling and Favourite Diversion of all Ranks of people from the Court to the Cottage in their different manners of Dancing'.

At this time new dances, collections of music and dances

purporting to be 'Caledonian' and 'Scotch' appeared in several books of the time, but printed in London.

Robert Walsh's *Caledonian Country Dances* which went into several editions in the 1740s did include genuine Scottish tunes but it was almost twenty years before a Scotsman, Robert Bremner, published in Edinburgh a collection of Scottish dance tunes, many of them hitherto unpublished traditional tunes, and popular reels and strathspeys. Bremner had turned the first furrow in the, as yet, barely explored hinterland of a fabulous musical heritage. After him a succession of publishers were to exploit the territory to the full.

Native tunes in reel-time became increasingly the music played for country dancing from the middle of the century onwards. And more and more often tunes of Scottish origin or in the Scottish style are found in manuals of country dancing in England and on the Continent in the second half of the 18th century. Bremner's dance tunes were avidly copied and imitated by contemporary printers and it is at this time that we find tunes frequently appearing in strathspey rhythm. Also, as the strathspey emerged and grew in popularity, dance progressions which had been danced in reel-time and to the country dance tunes were danced to strathspey rhythm. The differences in the dances then, as now, were only in their pace and the variations in the footwork demanded by the slower rhythm of the strathspey, not in their figures.

In Scotland the first dance title allusion to the strathspey is to be found in the Menzies Manuscript – a collection of dance figures without music, made in 1749. Incidentally, the earliest extant collection of Scottish dance tunes was that handwritten by David Young for the Duke of Perth in 1734.

In that same decade, the 1730s, the Edinburgh Assembly appears to have gone into something of a decline. Fashion is fickle and perhaps high society in Edinburgh had tired of dancing in the cramped and sometimes uncomfortable conditions offered by the Assembly Rooms. Even a move to different premises, a few closes down the High Street in 1736, failed to revive evidently flagging interest. Certainly the Assemblies had ceased altogether and, consequently, so had their subscriptions to charity by 1745. In that fatal year when Edinburgh was, for a brief few weeks, capital of a Jacobite kingdom there were no public Assemblies.

Charles Edward Stuart's arrival in Scotland and his march into Edinburgh, is the stuff of legend and was, in a very short time, the favourite subject of songwriters and composers. Close on their heels, exploiting the newly popular tunes and sentiments, were the compilers of country dances who soon were promoting dances with titles such as The White Cockade and Ye're Welcome Charley Stuart.

Incidentally, a young Atholl estate worker called Niel Gow, from Inver at Dunkeld, accompanied Bonnie Prince Charlie and Lord George Murray part of the way to Perth on the Jacobite march south. Had Niel Gow not thought the better of it and turned back for home there and then, Scottish music might have been the poorer through the loss on some southern battlefield of its finest and most famous fiddlers and composers!

In Edinburgh, the Jacobites triumphed and the gentry donned their white cockades and dancing shoes and danced with their prince in celebration. But not all of the city rose to the Stuart cause. Notably Provost George Drummond stood out against the prince and rode to Dunbar to offer his services to the Hanoverians. His 'sanity' in the face of the Jacobite hysteria that had swept his town, and his subsequent early return to office there, contributed much to Edinburgh's relatively speedy path back to normality after Jacobite triumph at Prestonpans led to the march on Derby and the run for home and Culloden.

There were, of course, many who could not resist a last flirtation with the romantic notion of 'the lad born to be king' and some Edinburgh ladies organized a Jacobite ball for an April evening in 1746. The ball, which began in great style with the news of an engagement between the Stuart and Hanoverian armies at Culloden, on Drummossie Moor, ended abruptly when the news of Cumberland's victory arrived.

Not long before Culloden, a meeting of eminent folk was held on 5 February 1746, with a view to re-establishing an Edinburgh Assembly. Among those present at that meeting were James Stirling, Treasurer of the Charity Workhouse, and Gavin Hamilton, Treasurer of the Royal Infirmary which had been under construction since 1738 and was now nearing completion.

The anxiety of these two men to restart the Assembly was surely not unconnected with their interest in fund-raising for their respective charities. The minute of that first meeting records, 'seeing that there had been no Assemblys for Dancing kept in Edinburgh for some considerable time the original design of which was a Fund for Charity, and being informed that Lady Orbistoun's Tack of the House called the New Assembly Hall where the Company used to Assemble was to expire at Whitsunday next', the gentlemen decided to sound out the possibility of renewing the lease and setting the town's feet dancing again for charity.

They took the lease of the house themselves 'at their own risque' for £50 sterling and for that sum the proprietor,

Roderick Chalmers, undertook to paint and whitewash the building, inside and out, and 'to mend all'.

On 20 May 1746, the new board of Directors met again to draw up the rules of the New Assembly. The conduct was to be pretty much as before:

'All dancing in the Assembly Hall and everything relating thereunto, shall be under the Inspection and manadgement of Ladies Directresses not exceeding seven who shall take their turn in the Direction Weekly, Monthly, or according as they shall agree it amongst themselves; the Lady Directress upon the night of her Manadgement to wear the Badge to be made for that purpose, and if it happen that the Lady who should direct for the night cannot attend she shall provide a Lady to take the Trouble for that night, who may be either one of the Directresses or any other lady she pleases to appoint, but she must give timely notice of the Lady's name to the Treasurer that he may send the badge unto her.'

The badge was evidently of importance to the performance of the office of Directress, which included, as before, the right to refuse admission to anyone who didn't measure up socially.

In November the Directors ordered to be made a 'badge of gold of an oval figure one side representing in Mezzo Relievo a Pelican upon her nest feeding her young, the motto Charity, and upon the reverse ingraven, the figure of a woman representing Charity leaning upon a Shield bearing the Arms of the Town of Edinburgh, a child leaning against her knee the motto upon an Escrole Edinburgh Assembly which badge to be worn by the Lady Directresses upon the night of her manadgement'.

The pelican symbol of charity was included in the arms adopted in 1749 by the committee of Edinburgh's new Infirmary and it appears today on the badge worn by nurses trained there – reference in tribute perhaps to the ladies of Edinburgh and the benificence of the Assemblies. Giving to the Infirmary, and to other charities, was, in fact, written into the Assembly's rules:

'That the Profites arising from the Assembly shall be divided into three equal shares, one whereof to be given to the Ladys Directresses to be by them bestowed in Publick or Private Charity as they shall think fit.' Over the years their contributions aided many objects of charity – from relief of the destitute to the construction of Kinghorn harbour.

'That another Share shall be paid into the Treasurer of the Royal Infirmary towards the support and maintenance of poor Patients lodged therein.

'That the third Share shall be paid into the Treasurer of the Charity Workhouse towards the support and maintenance of the Poor Lodged in the same.'

Edinburgh Royal Infirmary, being a main beneficiary of the Assembly, always had a representative on the board of Assembly Directors. When Gavin Hamilton resigned as Infirmary Treasurer in 1755, his successor was automatically made a Director of the Assembly which fact was duly noted in the minutes.

In addition to holding their own regular Assemblies, the Directors also sub-let the Assembly Hall 'at the rate of two guineas a night' to anyone wishing to avail themselves of the facilities, with the exception of the organizers of Charity Balls during the Assembly season. It is assumed that this was to prevent undue competition for funds. And in spite of subsequent applications to let the Hall for such balls, this rule was strictly adhered to – and a further thirty years were to pass before the Hall would also be let for afternoon card parties for charity during the Assembly season.

Arrangements for housekeeping and catering at the new Assemblies involved engaging someone at a salary of £15 per annum – a reduction in the salary paid previously – to attend to 'overseeing and manadging the work of the kitchen and serving the Company in the Assembly with Tea, Coffee etc. and keeping clean the House and Hall'. No fewer than two servants were to be kept and there were to be 'no Perquisites but the Profites of the Card Tables and of furnishing the company with Negus, Fruit and Cool Tankard, and not to exact above half a crown [12½ pence] for each pack of cards'.

The Treasurer was instructed to offer the above terms in the first instance to the 'Miss Robertsons, who have formerly, and are at present, employed in that way'. The 'Miss Robertsons' accepted the cut in salary and continued to serve the Assemblies until it was noted in the minutes of 22 March 1764 that one of them was dead and the other 'so old and infirm she was incapable of the duty and obliged to employ other low people who neglected it and kept the House very dirty'. The remaining Miss Robertson was pensioned off with a sum of £10 in August 1764 and thereafter received £8 per annum.

According to the rules of the Assembly the hiring and firing of servants and of musicians was left to the Gentlemen Directors. The Treasurer was given the task of making contracts with musicians on a sliding scale of pay according to attendance figures, and on promise of certain dismissal 'if they appear there in Drink or fail in giving punctual Attendance'.

The first Lady Directresses of the 1746 Assembly were the Countesses of Leven, Glencairn and Hopetoun, and the Ladies Minto and Middleton. It was up to them to set the tone of the Assembly and set out the rules for the conduct of an evening. Their rules were copied out and displayed in the Assembly Hall at their request. The rules, like the 'Miss Robertsons', served well and for long:

'No Lady to be admitted in a nightgown and no Gentleman in boots.

'Dancing to begin precisely at 5 o'clock afternoon in the winter and 6 o'clock in summer.

'Each set not to exceed ten couples to dance but one country dance at a time.

'The couples to dance their minuets in the order they stand in their several sets.

'No dancing out of regular order but by leave from the Lady Directress for the night.

'No dancing whatever to be allowed but in the ordinary dancing place.

'No dance to begin after 11 at night.

'No misses in skirts and jackets, robecoats nor stay-bodied gowns to be allowed to dance country dances but in a set by themselves.

'No tea, coffee, negus, nor other liquor to be carried into the dancing room.

'It is expected no gentleman will step over the rail round the dancing place, but will enter or go out by the doors at the upper or lower end of the room, and that all lady's and gentlemen will order their servants not to enter the passage before the outer door with lighted flambeaux.'

These rules were set in a gilded frame and hung in the entrance lobby of the Assembly Hall. As can be seen, they were principally designed for crowd control and to promote good behaviour in the comparatively confined space that the Assembly Room offered. People had to take it politely in turn to find space to dance.

Assemblies, thus conducted, were places where a mother would wish her daughter to be seen. There she might meet her contemporaries and equals with, perhaps, a matrimonial weather-eye open for a likely match in a place where all were thoroughly vetted and chaperoned.

It is not hard to imagine today, if one stands in Edinburgh's High Street and tries to forget the noise of traffic, how it must have been in the 1740s, 1750s and 1760s as the 'Flo'ers of Edinburgh' in all their finery and borne in sedan chairs, made their way at five o'clock of a winter's night to the Assembly Close. There would always have been a throng of spectators. In such an intimate, overcrowded place as Edinburgh's High Street, a braw show like an Assembly would have provided a splendid evening's entertainment for those outside as well as in. Crowds hung about the close all evening to hear the music and watch the comings and goings.

The Edinburgh Assembly became the hub of the Scottish gentry's social life, although the English writer, Oliver Goldsmith, visiting Edinburgh in 1753, found the dancing conducted so strictly as to be dull, and the company attending curiously unconvivial.

'When a stranger enters the dancing hall,' he wrote to a friend, 'he sees one end of the room taken up by the lady's who sit dismally in a Groupe by themselves. On the other end stand their pensive partners, that are to be, but no more intercourse between the sexes than there is between two Country's at war, the Ladies indeed may ogle and the Gentlemen sigh; but an embargo is laid on any closer commerce; . . .'

Scotland's gentry didn't find it so dull if their steady patronage of the Assembly is anything to judge by. The rooms were patently neither grand nor quite as the Assembly Directors would have wished, since on more than one occasion they asked the objects of their charity to agree to a suspension of payments in order to have ready funds for buying themselves a suitable property or for making improvements. They were constantly on the lookout for a new site and there was one proposal which almost came to fruition when they agreed with the Edinburgh Musical Society to build a hall suitable for both dancing and concerts. Sadly, nothing came of the plan. In the end they concentrated on spending a little money on decorations. In 1756 they spent £25 on four new lustres – chandeliers – and continued to dance in their cramped, stuffy rooms.

However, in the minutes of March 1759 the purchase of the hitherto rented Assembly Hall and Tavern for £1003 7s 9d is reported, and two years later land in an adjoining Wynd was purchased to allow the Directors to develop and expand. The Town Council gave their leave for the proposed development despite the fact the close would be darkened by new building, 'on the ground that so much comes to the Charity Workhouse, Royal Infirmary and Poor House'.

By 1766 a great rebuilding and refurbishing exercise was undertaken and some idea of the grandeur that was attained, in such an unlikely locale, may be gained today by visiting Edinburgh's Wax Museum which stands in the New Assembly Close and is all that remains of the building complex that grew up around the Old Assembly in 1766.

But, just as the beau monde of the High Street were settling into their renovated dancing quarters, moves were afoot that would, in time, transplant them from their Old Town tenements to a New Town of fine streets and squares.

In 1766 Edinburgh Town Council selected as the winner of
their competition for a New Town the plan of James Craig. The
Nor' Loch which had moated the Old Town was to be neatly
canalled and flanked with ornamental gardens and beyond was to
rise a new town which would provide dwellings more fit for
the men and women of the Golden Age.

In the meantime, before the New Town really got underway,
some speculative building was undertaken to the south and east
of the University in old Edinburgh. Some streets of elegant
houses and a couple of fine squares eased out from the centre of
the Old Town and many fashionable folk took their first leave of
the crowded towers of the High Street by moving into George's
Square and Nicolson Square and later to Buccleuch Place and
Buccleuch Street.

This movement outwards and away, affected the High Street
Assembly although it continued for some years and made
several serious attempts to adjust itself to new ways. The
afternoon card parties were begun and the Assembly rules
relaxed to accommodate the now fashionable later dining hours.

In 1773 the Directors ordained, 'that the present regulations be
taken down and copyd over with the following alterations, that
the hour to begin to dance shall be Six in winter and Seven in
summer and that the rule for not dancing after Eleven be left out,
and that matter be left entirely to the judgement of the Lady
Directrix for the night, that the number of couples to be allowed
to dance be augmented to twelve if the Lady Directrix thinks
proper, but the Managers recommend to the Lady Directrix
never to exceed that number'.

Thanks to one contemporary observer, an English captain,
Edward Topham, we have a full, if biased, record of Edinburgh's
fashionable life just before it departed the Old Town forever.

Dancing was still the principal recreation and was not confined
to Assemblies. Society balls and distinguished private dances
took place regularly throughout the season but there prevailed,
according to Topham, the same inhibited atmosphere, the same
reticence between the sexes as Goldsmith had remarked upon
twenty years before.

At the Assemblies, Topham noticed that in the confined space
so few could dance at the same time that those awaiting their
turn to take the floor had the perfect opportunity to chat
among themselves, to flirt a little, to strike up acquaintance.
That this did not happen was, Topham opined, due to a want of
gallantry on the part of 'Scotch Gentlemen' who did not avail
themselves of 'the finest opportunity they could wish as they are
left the whole evening to furnish entertainment and conversation
for their partners. But observations on the clothes and dancing

of the party who are performing, too often fill up the vacant interval and instead of ogling eyes, protestations and endearments, the lady sits envying the more fortunate stars of her companion who is dancing whilst her partner yawns for the approaching period of his own exhibition.'

Conversely, contemporary ladies have left accounts of these times as being Edinburgh's gayest and most sociable.

Topham also noted, 'the gravest of men here, with the exception of the ministers, think it no disgrace to dance. I have seen a professor, who has argued most learnedly and most wisely in the morning, forgetting all his gravity in an evening and dancing away to the best of his abilities.'

Perhaps Topham did not remain long enough in Scotland to appreciate a facet of the Lowland Scottish character which does not equate gaiety and sociability with ogling and empty love talk! And the men he watched standing around lacking in gallantry counted among their number some of the finest brains of the day with more to concern them than paying idle court to a lady!

He did stop long enough, though, to note how much more enlivened the Edinburgh dancers were by the sound of their native music and dances, the Threesome and Foursome reels, than by the figures of the minuet and the country dance.

He wrote: 'The general dance here is the reel which requires that particular sort of steps to dance properly of which none but the people of the country have any idea. The perseverence which the Scotch ladies discover in these reels is not the less surprising than their attachment to them in preference to all others. They will sit totally unmoved at the most sprightly airs of an English country dance, but the moment one of these [reel] tunes is played, which is liquid laudanum to my spirits, up they start, animated with new life, and you would imagine they had been bit by a tarantula. These tunes were originally performed on the bagpipe.'

In the preceding ten years, Robert Bremner and his successors had produced a series of collections of old tunes, some adapted for the fiddle from pipe music and rendered suitable for dancing. What began as a trickle of tunes, turned into a full-scale flood of adaptations, realizations and imitations resulting in a general revival of interest in Scotland's native music. The movement reached its triumphant climax with the superb adaptations and revivals of old songs undertaken by Robert Burns in the 1780s.

'The effect which these national dances have,' continued observer Topham, 'and the partiality which many natives discover for them, is certainly a matter of great surprise to a stranger. The young people of England only consider dancing an agreeable means of bringing them together. But the Scotch admire the reel for its own merit alone, and may truly be said to dance for the sake of dancing.

'A Scotsman comes into an assembly-room as he would into a field of exercise, dances till he is literally tired, possibly without ever looking at his partner, or almost knowing who he dances with. In most countries the men have a partiality for dancing with a woman; but here I have frequently seen four gentlemen perform one of these reels seemingly with the same pleasure and perseverence as they would have done, had they the most sprightly girl for a partner. They give you the idea that they could with equal glee cast off round a joint stool or set to a corner cupboard.'

Topham was doubtless unaware of the Kirk's dislike of promiscuous dancing which had given rise to the practice of Scotsmen frequently dancing together, but he couldn't have been unaware of traditional dances, such as Morris dances, for men only in his own country. What seems to have been remarkable to him was the interchangeable nature of the traditional reel which could be danced by three or four people, by one sex or the other or a mixture of the two, and with a variety of steps.

By Topham's time, the Threesome and Foursome Reels had become the mixture of strathspey and reel rhythm and steps familiar today. And there was also a form of Twosome danced in strathspey rhythm, in regular use at the Assemblies – Topham reported: 'Another of their national dances is a kind of quick minuet or what the Scotch call a Straspae. We in England are said to walk a minuet; this is galloping a minuet. The French one is esteemed by all people at the Opera as particularly elegant, and affording the greatest opportunity possible for a fine woman to display her figure to advantage. In this of the Scotch, however, every idea of grace seems inverted, and the whole is a burlesque.

'Nothing of the minuet is presented except the figure; the steps and time most resemble a hornpipe – and I leave you to dwell on the picture of a gentleman fully-dressed and a lady in a hoop, lappets, and every other incumbrance of ornament, dancing a hornpipe before a large assembly.'

A closer examination of Topham's description of the 'galloping minuet' with the minuet figure intact, brings to mind strongly the Highland Schottische, immensely popular in Victorian times, and still taught as a ballroom dance today. Despite the German sound of the title 'Schottische', the Highland Schottische can perhaps claim its origins in Topham's 'Straspae'.

By the 1770s, as evidenced by Topham's visit, the English were beginning to overcome their anti-Scottishness, a sentiment rife since the '45, and were coming north of the Border to see for themselves the 'wild' country which was producing some of the most eminent thinkers of the day.

Soon feeling against the Scots was replaced by a positive vogue for things Scottish, and Scottish dances and dance music became very popular at English Assemblies.

Robert Bremner, the Edinburgh publisher, was now in London 'at the sign of the Harp and Hautboy in the Strand', doing first-class business with collections of Scots songs, marches and airs, and his *Scots Reels and Country Dances* which included popular dances like Tullochgorm, The Birks of Abergeldy, and various strathspeys with the caution: '(N.B. – the strathspey reels are played much slower than the others.)'

Ladies Repositories, tiny handbooks-cum-diaries-cum-encyclopedias which appeared in the middle of the 18th century, containing such essentials as the new songs at Vauxhall, new rules to be observed at Bath, shopping advice and information on child ailments, also contained the titles and instructions for the year's new country dances. In *The Ladies Complete Pocket Book* of 1768, published in London, only two titles seem as though they might have a Scottish connection – Miss Poultenay's Delight and Miss Bryce's Delight. However, a little later there is a fair sprinkling of 'new' Scottish dances appearing each year with titles such as Mrs McLeod of Rousa, The Highland Fair, Lady Matilda Bruce's Reel.

In France, too, things Scottish and pseudo-Scottish were in considerable vogue. The queen, Marie Antoinette, loved to dance Ecossaises and had two notable Scottish partners with whom she used to indulge this fancy. The Ecossaise as a dance has so far defied attempts at exact identification. Some hold that it was simply a country dance performed in the Scottish manner, that is, with Scottish steps and tunes; others, that an Ecossaise was a dance of entirely French origin performed to tunes with no perceptible Scottish influence, awarded the title merely because of the fashion for Scottishness.

If the latter is the case, then it is strange to find the Scottish Lord Strathaven the subject of gossip at the French court as being the queen's too frequent partner in Ecossaises at private parties. Was it likely she'd have selected *him* to partner her in dances of purely French origin? It seems much more likely that the French court had adopted the Scottish manner of doing country dances – and Lord Strathaven probably delighted in the chance to show off his studied footwork.

There is a distinct possibility that the Scottish vogue at the

French court had begun when Lord Stormont, heir to the first
Earl Mansfield, had been British Ambassador to the court from
1772–8. Lord Stormont's aunt, Miss 'Nicky' Murray, was a
famous Edinburgh Assembly Directress of the time. Stormont
and his pretty young second wife had been particular
favourites of the French queen who showered them with gifts in
token of her deep affection. What more natural than that the
queen should extend her enthusiasm to dancing in the Scottish
style which the Stormonts demonstrated to her? The French
royal family and the court at Versailles, on their inexorable
descent to oblivion, were perpetually avid for novelty.

Country dances at that time were very much the fashion in
France and dancing teachers and publishers there did a roaring
trade in 'new' dances and books of music and instruction. The
nobility made, as always in France, an art of dancing. It was
something to be assiduously studied and practised.

Keen students collected books of instruction for popular
dances and there exists today, in the International Dance
Archives housed in the Library of the Paris Opéra, a superb
collection of 18th-century aides-mémoires and country dance
collections – some of them perfectly shaped to slip into an
elegant pocket.

The French had also developed a country-dance form, the
cotillon, which began as a dance for four couples in a square set
and was developed in Victorian times, in this country and in
North America, into a sort of round-the-room dance during which
there was progressive changing of partners – the precursor of the
barn dances of North America.

The square-dance cotillon was reported by Topham as being
unknown in Edinburgh in 1775 but, although it was introduced a
short time later by a dancing master, it didn't appear to gain
much popularity north of the Border.

In the 1780s, however, there was more than a new dance or
two afoot in Edinburgh. Over in the rapidly growing New Town,
in 1783, the foundation stone of the George Street Assembly
Rooms was laid. Here, at last, would be room enough to dance in
a setting as modern and elegant as could be devised.

But neither Edinburgh's fashionables nor their Assembly made
the change from the High Street to the New Town in one move –
both took a sideways step. Just as the professors, the gentry,
and the judges had moved first to live on the south side of the
University, so did the Assembly.

The George (originally George's) Square Assembly was begun
in 1785, and the old Assembly Rooms in the High Street were
sold to the Town Council later in the year to be fitted up as
lodging for the Town Guard. The furniture and lustres were

disposed of, the latter being presented to the Gentlemen of Fife, in 1790, for the Cupar Assembly Rooms.

At first in the George Square Assembly, the former style of Assembly dancing was preserved and conduct was according to the laws of Nash, but times were changing. According to new regulations, twenty-four Assemblies were to be held weekly on Wednesday, 'the one week for dancing, and the other for cards, beginning with a Dancing Assembly – the hour of meeting to be half past six, and of dismissing not later than one in the morning'.

Still there seems to have been a problem of space, 'the number of couples in each set to be regulated by the Lady Directress; and those who have been in the preceeding set shall give place to the other Ladies and Gentlemen who chuse to dance in the following set; and so alternately'. There was to be no dancing of reels during the country dances – an indication both of the lack of space and of the happy interchangeability of the music for reels and country dances. But the George Square Assembly was highly successful, if short lived, and under constant pressure from rival Assemblies.

Henry Cockburn, the eminent Law Lord who lived from 1779–1854, writing in *Memorials of His Time*, published in 1856, left behind the perfect valediction to the George Square Assembly. And what he wrote could equally well have applied to the High Street days, long past, when Ladies Orbistoun and Drumelzier and the Countesses of Leven and Hopetoun reigned.

'The ancient dancing establishments in the Bow and the Assembly Close I know nothing about. Everything of the kind was meant to be annihilated by the erection of the handsome apartments in George Street. Yet even against these, the new part of the Old Town made a gallant struggle, and in my youth the whole fashionable dancing, as indeed the fashionable everything, clung to George Square; where in Buccleuch Place, (close by the south-eastern corner of the square) most beautiful rooms were erected, which, for several years, threw the New Town piece of presumption entirely into the shade. And here were the last remains of the ballroom discipline of the preceding age. Martinet dowagers and venerable beaux acted as masters and mistresses of ceremonies and made all the preliminary arrangements. No couple could dance unless each party was provided with a ticket prescribing the precise place in the precise dance. If there was no ticket, the gentleman, or the lady, was dealt with as an intruder, and turned out of the dance.

'If the ticket had marked upon it – say for a country dance, the figures 3.5; this meant that the holder was to place himself in the third dance and fifth from the top; and if he was anywhere else, he was set right, or excluded. And the partner's ticket must correspond. Woe on the poor girl who with ticket 2.7, was found opposite a youth marked 5.9! It was flirting without a license, and looked very ill, and would probably be reported by the ticket director to the mother. Of course parties, or parents, who wished to secure dancing for themselves or those they had charge of, provided themselves with correct and corresponding vouchers before the ball day arrived. This could only be accomplished through a director; and the election of a pope sometimes required less jobbing.

'When parties chose to take their chance, they might do so; but still, though only obtained in the room, the written permission was necessary; and such a thing as a compact to dance, by a couple, without official authority, would have been an outrage that could scarcely be contemplated.'

The prissiness of such behaviour makes odd companion to some of the tune titles to which they danced the night away, titles such as Geld Him Lasses, O If I had such a Lassie as This, Haud the Lass Till I Winn at Her, and I Wish You would Marry Me Now.

Many of the country dances which have been revived in the present day, date from this time, but those lost for ever are without number.

Ordinarily at an Assembly a Master of Ceremonies was appointed to call out the dances, rather in the fashion of a modern American square dance caller. If the chosen dance were familiar, he would simply call out the title and an occasional figure or two such as 'Advance, retire, set, turn all, hands round' whenever confusion seemed imminent in the sets. But he was also expected to call up new dances which he might either create on the spot, or devise in the course of the days between Assemblies, introducing them when the opportunity arose. If such a dance included a good and enjoyable series of figures, it might be performed over and over until it was thoroughly well known to the company. It would either be named after the tune to which it was danced, such as The Lea Rig or Jenny Dang the Weaver, or named after a current event, or a popular public figure destined to pass into posterity as the name in the title of a dance. Among such were the Misses Clemy Stewart, Welsh, Burns, the Lady Jean Murray and Lady Auckland, all of whom had dances named after them.

A title such as The Duchess of Atholl's Slipper is tantalizing. This dance is named after a tune by Niel Gow which he, in turn, had named after the footwear of his employer's wife. But, sadly, the story of how the Duchess came to have a tune dedicated to one of her slippers, we shall never know.

The Duchess of Gordon's Fancy is another dance of that time named after a lady – in this instance a well-known personage. Jane, Duchess of Gordon, was, in the latter half of the 18th century, a central figure in Edinburgh's social life and, indeed, in London's too. She was an avid dancer who footed reels well into her old age. (It was, incidentally, to the George Square Assembly, that the Duchess convoyed Robert Burns during his triumphant first visit, in 1786, to the capital.)

Cockburn tells us that the New Town 'altered the style of living, obliterated local arrangements, and destroyed a thousand associations, which nothing but the still preserved names of houses and places is left to recall'.

The George Street Assembly rooms in the New Town were officially opened for the Caledonian Hunt Ball on 11 January 1787, though the rooms were barely complete for the occasion. Robert Burns was still in town, supervising the publication of the Edinburgh Edition of his poems. The gentlemen of the Caledonian Hunt, to whom the Edition was dedicated, had subscribed towards one hundred copies of the work and Burns, in the course of his stay in the city, had become acquainted with a number of the gentlemen. It was the son of one of these, Sir John Whitefoord, that Burns described as being 'in a fuss today, like a coronation – this is the great day – the Assembly and ball of the Caledonian Hunt; and John has had the good luck to pre-engage the hand of the beauty-famed and wealth-celebrated Miss McAdam . . .'

The new Assembly Rooms were, according to a newspaper account of the opening, the largest in Britain, 'except the Great Room at Bath, and is said to exceed it in elegance and just proportion – the building of the rooms etc. has cost about eight thousand pounds. The opening was a triumph with about three hundred and forty attending, including 'all the people of fashion in the town'.

The rules of the new Edinburgh Assembly using the George Street Rooms were drawn up in apparent preoccupation with appearances:

'No young lady out of woman's dress to be allowed to dance.
'No young gentleman with his hair untied, or without powder, to be permitted to dance.
'No gentleman will be admitted in boots or with a stick.
'It is expected that no person will come to the assemblies improperly dressed.'

Spaciousness in the New Town was not confined to the new Assembly Rooms. Private houses were now commodious affairs with plenty of space for giving private parties, and entertaining at home became both practical and pleasurable.

Once removed from the confines of the High Street and the inevitable intimacy with all ranks and conditions of folk, the denizens of the New Town became perhaps less aware of those dependent upon their charity. Whatever the reasons, the Assembly in the New Town never attained the popularity that the Assembly had enjoyed in the earlier part of the century. Soon the beautiful Assembly Rooms were to witness no more regular Assemblies but they serve to this day as Edinburgh's principal venue for occasional balls and fashionable functions.

All over Scotland, not just in Edinburgh, people were beginning to dance at home rather than at Assemblies. The wealthy and growing middle class were providing themselves with houses large enough to entertain in as well as to live in. Assembly Rooms gave way to drawing rooms.

Cockburn recorded that the move to Edinburgh's New Town radically changed 18th-century Edinburgh. Industrialization, too, was making its black, smoke-laden mark on the countryside. Other cities were growing, and great influxes of Highland labour were already bursting Glasgow's bustling seams.

The end of the century was a time of political and economic turbulence with much talk of revolution. Successive wars with France put the entire country on a military footing with The Volunteer Militia drilling on links and village commons.

Minuets, with all their stateliness and grace were out of step with this life and, despite the dance's enduring favour with the dancing masters as the supreme dance for inculcating dignity and grace, it had all but disappeared from the social scene. With it, something of the Golden Age also departed, and not only from Edinburgh.

In Dundee in 1799, it was complained, 'the elegance of the ancient dancing assemblies is gone! and in its place are introduced card playing! and a warming reel before departure'.

But in spite of the loss of elegance, Assemblies in the lesser cities and burghs of Scotland continued well into the 19th century and a contemporary account has it that in Dundee they 'were very exclusive, those only who had been subscribers to them being admitted, but an exception was made in favour of the officers of any regiment stationed in Dundee at the time, or any gentleman from the country', – these balls were held in the Town Hall with one of the large adjoining rooms set apart as a card room. However, even the so-called large rooms were barely large enough, and complaints abounded about the cramped conditions. 'Advanced as we now are in wealth, refinement and luxury, it is to be regretted that in Dundee no better dancing rooms can be procured. Even fifty years ago they might have been reckoned incommodious.'

In spite of the common complaint that the elegance of former days had gone, Scotland *was* now considerably more advanced in 'wealth, refinement and luxury' than she had ever been before and, as far as dancing was concerned, it was Scotland's turn to dominate the ballrooms of England and Europe.

Country dances were danced to Scottish tunes. Threesome and Foursome Reels, Scotland's truly native dances, had become by the 1790s among the most popular dances of the fashionable world – and that included the fashionable of young America, who continued to dance the old dances of 'home' to which, in time, they would add the overlay of a new, independently produced culture.

Edinburgh's dancing masters were so numerous as to constitute a major industry in the town, and to them flocked dancing teachers from every airt. As one dancing master wrote: 'It is no uncommon thing, at Edinburgh, to see men of our profession who come there with no other view, but to acquire a knowledge of the proper steps made use of in that dance [The Scotch Reel as it was now dubbed]. It is not long since that two of them, father and son, came from London to Edinburgh for no other purpose; and as they had their own carriage, it may be presumed they must have been men of some reputation in their profession.

'They made application to the most fashionable teacher of dancing in that place.' Thereupon the London dancers undertook a rigorous course of three lessons a day to learn the steps of the Scotch Reels, signifying 'the importance they thought a right knowledge of the dance in question might do them on their return to London'.

And all through this era country dances were continuing to please and to be polished, changed, refined to suit the mode of the day. It was, for instance, just before the end of the century that the poussette and the allemande were introduced to supplement the traditional crossing over or casting off as a means of moving down the dance.

It is to the credit of Edinburgh that, when such opportunity existed for parvenues and fly-by-night teachers to set up in business, they were almost always quickly exposed and prised out of business. The good teachers included in their number some first-class musicians who were regular orchestral performers giving concerts in the Musical Society's St Cecilia's Hall. One of their number, James Oswald, became Chamber Composer to George III.

Edward Topham noted how vital the Scots felt a musical education to be as well as learning to dance. As a result a master who could impart a knowledge of both was at a considerable advantage in earning a living over one who based his dance prospectus merely on declarations of visits to London and Paris to learn new dances. What need had the Athens of the North of new dances from London and Paris, when their dancing masters flocked here to learn ours!

But, before long, the Scotch Reels, even the country dances, were to be swept out of all Europe's ballrooms. All Europe, that is, except for Scotland. Times and fashions were to change, but the strong Scottish taste for good footwork and neat steps was to ensure the survival of the old dances.

The music emanating from the bows and pens of Niel Gow and his family, of the Duff brothers, of William Marshall of Fochabers, and a multitude of others, would continue to enrich the musical treasury of Scotland beyond measure. And the study and practice of dancing would continue to be held a necessary part of education for another century to come.

5

THE SCIENTIFIC PROFESSORS

Although, for over a century, Edinburgh had been the focus of dancing activity in Scotland, it was not, as we have already seen, the only place where Scots danced and studied the art. Throughout the country, dancing masters, or dancies as they were called in the east and north east, were hard at work teaching new dances and attempting to inculcate some kind of grace and decorum into old reels and new pupils.

It is not possible to praise enough nor to pay too much attention to the activities of the dancies whose profession went from strength to strength throughout the 19th and into the early 20th centuries. Their influence has declined only well within living memory.

At the beginning of the 19th century, Francis Peacock – who would have been, no doubt, somewhat annoyed to have been called a 'dancie' – was the official town dancing master of Aberdeen. He was appointed to that post in 1747 and held it till his death in 1807.

Francis Peacock is important to the dance story on several counts, not least of which is his lasting reputation as an example of the finest sort of dancing master. He was a thorough scholar in his profession, publishing books of music and dance instruction and entering fully into the cultural life of the city which employed him.

Aberdeen, too, has a particular place in the story of dancing in Scotland. It was, during the Reformation, the centre of much counter-Reformation activity and, when the dust finally settled, a great many of the leading families of the north east – the Hays, the Forbes's and the Setons and Gordons – had remained Roman Catholic or had adopted the English Reformed Church. As a consequence of this, there remained in the north east far longer than elsewhere, traces of the old rural customs and attitudes, and the stern rule of the Kirk did not have the same strait-lacing effect on the people there.

Dancing had always been an important part of Aberdeen's life. Burgh records from medieval times contain many references to town ceremonials and to holidays celebrated with official dancing. Therefore it is no surprise to find Aberdeen with a town dancing master who had responsibility for running the 'Publick Balls of dancing in this place' as early as 1695.

Before Francis Peacock was appointed to the position, the town had, apparently, had difficulty in finding a dancing master to its liking. Although the Kirk didn't have too much sway and say in the running of things in Aberdeen, the Town Council did, and had the best interests of its folk at heart. In 1742, the townsfolk, recognizing that 'the town was at a great loss for want of a right dancing-master to educate their children,' put pressure on the Council to find a master.

The result was an advertisement inviting all who felt themselves suitably qualified 'to come to Aberdeen the twelfth of August next, there to take tryall of their qualifications and who is found the best qualified to have the sole and exclusive privilege of being a Dancing Master within the Burgh and that during his good behaviour'.

The upshot was, in best Aberdonian tradition, a free dancing display by two applicants before a crowd of the town's gentry. The applicants demonstrated teaching methods as well as their own dancing abilities, and finally one, James Stuart from Montrose, was chosen.

The Council's rules, set down for Stuart's personal conduct and the conduct of his classes, must be taken to reflect the problems previously encountered by the Council. It was ordered:

'That he take no apprentices to teach privately without their masters' knowledge.

'That he behave before his scholars and all other companie in a decent manner as becomes a teacher of youth, abstaining from swearing or any other immorrall practices.

'That he shall not haunt taverns with his scholars or drink with them in the same unless it be by permission of their parents or masters, or when any of them is alongst with their children or apprentices.

'That at the hour he appoint his scholars to meet he duly attend so as to prevent disorder amongst them.

'That his fees to teach dancing shall be six shillings and eight pence [33½ pence] sterling per month.'

Whether James Stuart measured up or not we don't know, but he didn't last long since, in 1747, Francis Peacock was appointed 'to be sole dancing master within the burgh during his good behaviour'. He came from Edinburgh to Aberdeen with splendid character references and in the succeeding sixty years he exemplified what a town dancing master should be.

We can judge the manner of his conduct of classes from the

account of a contemporary and pupil, Alexander Jaffray of Kingswells, in whose *Recollections of 1755-1800* we find this:

'I attended the established dancing school of the city. The master was Mr. Peacock, a really scientific professor. He was, of course, an excellent master, but stern and severe when a dull pupil came under his hands. I went through the minuet, but very indifferently, and declined exhibiting at the Ball, finding myself unequal to the task. The only part I took any pleasure in was the country dancing practised once a week.'

By the time Alexander Jaffray attended Peacock's classes they were being held in his permanent dancing school built just off the city's Castlegate. And it wasn't likely that Jaffray was a favourite pupil of Francis Peacock, since the latter believed firmly that the most important dance a master could teach was the minuet.

As for Jaffray's favourite country dancing – Peacock much preferred to teach the Scotch Reel rather than country dances 'whose jigging parts and figures of the dance I count little or nothing'.

We know exactly what Peacock taught and his thoughts on the art of dancing from his book published in 1805, two years before his death. Entitled *Sketches Relative to the History, Theory, but more especially to the Practice of Dancing,* it sets down his observations on the teaching of dancing and above all the glories of the minuet.

'My chief aim,' the book begins, 'is to give my sentiments on the advantages arising to youth, from their being well instructed in the Minuet; a dance essentially necessary for them to learn, on account of its utility, as a foundation for the superstructure of those graces which distinguish people of fashion, and good breeding, from others whose education has been neglected, or their manners perverted by bad teachers.'

In the years preceding the publication of Peacock's book, there had been a steady stream of books of Scottish dances produced by a variety of genuine teachers, and also charlatans and copyists out to make a killing in a popular market. Peacock's book is remarkable not only for the quality of the treatment of his subject, but because he is the very first dance writer to set down detailed instructions for steps of the Scotch Reel as taught by him.

It is an example of the best of the good dance manuals and is a significant landmark in the story of dancing in Scotland. In a series of short chapters which Peacock called Sketches, he sets down his thoughts on everything from doffing a hat and handing a gift, to physiotherapy and the wearing of a brace to correct round shoulders.

But it is on dancing that he is at his most interesting, his most revealing. Through him we can try to visualize what it was the good dancing master asked of his pupils, and we can imagine, considering the natural waywardness of youth in every generation, how dedicated a dancing master had to be to instil any of Peacock's ideals in his dancing class pupils. Consider, for instance, what he required of a minuet.

'There are some pointed traits in a just and elegant performance of the Minuet, as well as in all other school dances which ought to be attended to with precision; such as a well-set Head, an expressive modesty in the Eye, and a diversity of Countenance; the inflextions of the Neck, which should be free and easy; the Shoulders well drawn back, and a full chest; a graceful and dignified carriage of the Body; a gentle commanding flexibility of the Joints in sinking and rising; the good position, and proportionate distance of the Feet, in all their motions; a free, yet nervous play of the Instep.

'These, together with a graceful management of the Arms, and manner of giving the Hands, are the outlines of a portrait, which require little more than the aid of an able artist to complete.'

Peacock admits perfection is hard to come by – rare, 'indeed few are to be met with who are endued with all the properties necessary to the perfection of Dancing, nor can this be looked for'. He does admit, however, that sometimes a good appearance and the right mood can compensate for defective footwork, but that was no reason to give up striving for perfection in dancing. And one may easily imagine from Jaffray's description the earnestness with which Peacock went about his work, 'a really scientific professor . . . stern and severe when a dull pupil came under his hands'.

Alexander Jaffray put up with the Peacock regime for three months only and it seems he was not alone. Peacock admits as much in his book.

'It is indeed with regret I have observed for many years past the Minuet has almost totally fallen into disuse in our public assemblies; a circumstance I cannot otherwise account for, than by supposing it is, in a great measure, owing to the gentlemen not keeping pace with the ladies, in the fashionable improvements of this dance – the gentlemen seldom pay the smallest attention to it after they leave school, perhaps at the early period of thirteen or fourteen years of age; while the ladies, on the contrary, continue to improve in it, till they are sixteen or seventeen, when they are introduced into the assemblies of fashion from the hands of their teachers.'

Peacock proved such a paragon of all the virtues Aberdeen could have wished for in an official dancing master, it seems, that the conduct of assemblies was left to him, although that did not mean that the charitable aspect of assemblies was forgotten. Indeed, Francis Peacock donated the proceeds of the sale of the *Sketches* to Aberdeen's newly built Lunatic Hospital.

The conduct of Aberdeen's assemblies under Peacock involved, according to Jaffray, 'the gentlemen inviting a lady to be his evening's partner in advance of the event, meeting her at the Assembly Rooms, and having had their sets and places appointed to them, they remained partners for the evening'.

Dancing was followed by supper and the ladies were then escorted home, the gentlemen returning later to drink the ladies' healths. The last custom followed the fashion in Edinburgh where, by the end of the century, it was the habit of the gentlemen, having escorted their ladies home, to rendezvous at some appointed howff in order to drink what was left of the night away.

As well as teaching them to dance, conducting their assemblies and correcting the physical defects in their young, Peacock also enriched the Aberdonians' social life in his enthusiasm and work for the city's Musical Society and as an artist and miniaturist of note.

Today, Francis Peacock, who served his city so well and featured so large in its cultural life, has but one memorial. His name graces the alleyway in the Castlegate where his dancing school once stood – Peacock's Close it remains.

By the time Peacock wrote his *Sketches* in 1805, the minuet had almost vanished from the dance assemblies although, in Aberdeen and Dundee and in the countryside, the dancing masters continued to teach it in various guises well into the 19th century.

Mr McLagan, a Dundee dancing master, regularly headed the list of dances in his prospectus with the minuet until 1840. And in the same city a prospectus, published in 1892 for Mr Albert Johnstone, announces that he will teach the 'Sword Dance, Highland Fling, Seann Trubhais, Hieland Laddie, Reel Steps, Sailor's Hornpipe, Irish Jig and Variety Hornpipe, also Minuettes for Ladies'.

Apart from teaching deportment, country dancing and the minuet, a dancing master such as Francis Peacock was certainly much employed teaching the so-called 'High' dances – the solo and step dances – much developed by the Edinburgh dancing masters in the 18th century.

From time to time Francis Peacock placed an announcement in the local press that he was out of town 'in order to acquaint himself with the new dances which he hopes may please those who propose to do him the honour of attending his school the ensuing summer'.

The High dances were arranged or composed mainly to give individual pupils of ability the opportunity to perform solos, pas de deux, or pas de trois and so on at the dancing classes' regular exhibitions – a form of advertising for future pupils that no dancing master then, or since, has been able to dispense with.

Most of these High dances specially composed for exhibitions exist today only in lists of titles. And from these lists we learn nothing of the dances themselves, simply the names of the pupils for whom they were written.

One solo dance which has come down to us with its tune and choreography, is entitled The Earl of Errol. The earl, Lord High Constable of Scotland, was a pupil and friend of Francis Peacock who may have composed this dance for him to perform. But dances such as the Pas Seul for Miss Margaret Burnett of Leys, and the Pas de Deux for the Misses Grant of Monymusk have gone forever. The latter two were compositions of Archibald Duff, assistant to and successor of Peacock.

Many solo dances employed very intricate, balletic steps often performed with such skill as to astonish the onlooker. A visiting Irishman in Edinburgh was heard to exclaim at one such exhibition: 'I never saw children so handy with their feet.'

The teaching of such 'handiness' was begun at a very early age and we are indebted to Francis Peacock for having written down in his *Sketches* the kind of steps taught for the Scotch Reel, since these steps were also often used, with adaptation and embellishment, as the basis of steps for the solo dances.

That the steps taught for the Scotch Reel had their origins in the Highlands is difficult to dispute, and it is significant that all the steps which Peacock lists have names in anglicized Gaelic. Kemshoole for *ceum siubhail*, the forward step; kemkossy for *ceum coiseachadh*, the setting step; lematrast for *leum trasd*, cross springs; and so on. In each case, Peacock uses the 'Gaelic' name although he sprinkles his explanations with French ballet terms.

Peacock, a great admirer of the footwork of native Highland dancers, wrote: 'I once had the pleasure of seeing, in a remote part of the country, a Reel danced by a herd boy and two young girls, who surprised me much, especially the boy, who appeared to be about twelve years of age. He had a variety of well chosen steps, and executed them with so much justness and ease, as if he meant to set criticism at defiance. Circumstances like these plainly evince, that those qualities must either be inherent in the Highlander or that they must have an uncommon aptitude for imitation.

'Our colleges draw hither, every year, a number of students

from the Western Isles, as well as from the Highlands, and the greater part of them excel in this dance [the Scotch Reel]; some of them, indeed, in so superior a degree, that I myself have thought them worthy of imitation.'

No doubt Peacock was not alone in his appreciation of Highland steps and it is hardly surprising, therefore, that step and High dances which survived and passed into the dancing masters' permanent repertoire would include titles like the Highland Fling, Lochaber Broadswords, Highland Laddie, the Ghillie Callum, and Seann Trubhais. And, given the importance and the enthusiasm of dancing masters like Francis Peacock, there can be little doubt that step dances of native Highland origin underwent considerable changes in their development and acceptance in the Lowland dancing salons.

Elizabeth Grant of Rothiemurchus in Strathspey, whose delightful autobiography *Memoirs of a Highland Lady* contains many allusions to dancing in the early years of the 19th century, writes thus of the activities of a country dancie in her area:

'A dancing master taught us every variety of wonderful Highland step – that is, he taught me, for William never could learn anything, though he liked hopping about to the fiddle – and we did "Merrily danced the Quaker's wife" together, quite to the satisfaction of the servants, who all took lessons too, in common with the rest of the population, the Highlanders considering this art an essential in the education of all classes, and never losing an opportunity of acquiring a few more flings and shuffles. The dancing master had, however, other most distinguished pupils, the present Duke of Manchester, and his elder sister Lady Jane Montague, who were then living in our close neighbourhood with their grandmother the Duchess of Gordon.' (The Duchess of Gordon was the splendid Duchess Jane who had lionized Burns in Edinburgh and who continued to love dancing almost to her dying day.)

Not only did the grand and the ordinary folk share a teacher in order to learn additional 'flings and shuffles', but often, to the astonishment of visitors to rural Scotland at the time, they shared ballrooms.

Elizabeth Grant continues her account: 'We were often over at Kinrara, the Duchess [of Gordon] having perpetual dances, either in the drawing room or the servants' hall, and my father returning these entertainments in the same style. A few candles lighted up bare walls at short warning, fiddles and whisky punch were always at hand, and the gentles and simples reeled away in company.'

At private parties such as these, solo dance displays gave the general body of dancers a breather.

'We children sometimes displayed our accomplishments on these occasions in a prominent manner, to the delight, at any rate, of our dancing master. Lady Jane was really clever in the Ghillie Callum and the Shean Trews, I little behind her in the single and double fling, the shuffle and heel-and-toe step. The boys were more blundering, and had to bear the good-natured laugh of many a hard-working lass and lad who, after the toil of the day, footed it neatly and lightly in the ballroom till near midnight.'

Lady Jane's expertise at the 'Ghillie Callum and Shean Trews' offers an interesting mention of these dances whose origins are obscure but whose development by the dancing masters brought them to the forefront – a place they still retain in the official Highland dance repertoire.

With the passing of time and for want of any real authority on their history, some of our best-loved solo dances have gathered round them all sorts of daft and romantic legends in an effort to fill the gaps in real knowledge. Seann Trubhais has gathered its share of these; such as tales that the dance is symbolic of disaffected Highlanders kicking off the trews they were forced to wear when kilt and tartan were banned after the '45 rebellion, all of which must be completely discounted since trews were common garb among Highlanders long before the Jacobite era.

All that is certain about the dance is that its theme is old trousers, that it used to be a very merry, probably a comic, dance with much more pantomime in it, which puts it into the ancient pantomime dance tradition. It was the dancing masters who rendered it gradually into the graceful dance it has become – a dance suitable for Lady Jane and succeeding cohorts of little girls to perform.

The Ghillie Callum with its crossed swords is redolent of a variety of ancient dance traditions – dances before battle, dances celebrating victory, dances in which the swords display the sign of the cross. Whatever its origins, it has been the delight of dancing masters for two hundred years and more to teach pupils of both sexes the nimble footwork involved in dancing over crossed swords without touching the blades.

There is no record of exactly when the Ghillie Callum entered the dancing classrooms but for many years this dance had been one of the attractions of the Lowland cattle trysts, particularly the Falkirk Tryst, when Highland drovers, at the end of a week's trading, gathered together to try each other in feats of strength and in dancing and piping.

From the competitions at these trysts grew the Lowland 'Highland' Games, and the piping and dancing competitions sponsored by the Highland Societies of London and Edinburgh, which were founded towards the end of the 18th century.

During the 19th century at 'Highland' Games held all over the country, the dancing competitions were of equal importance and interest to spectators and competitors as the athletic feats. Many notable athletes were also dancers of renown. Today, so often, the dancing platform is simply the territory of child performers and few, if any, competitors in the field and track events could, or would, participate in the dance competitions.

The Scottish regiments, too, contributed their share to the history of competitive dances. Regimental records of service in all corners of the British Empire also include reports of Highland Division Games in venues from Guinea to Poona, Bridge of Don to Bloemfontein. Regular inter-company dance competitions were held and at inter-regimental Highland Games, dancing was an important part of a day's events. The principal dances performed were Foursome Reels, the Highland Fling and Ghillie Callum.

The music for these dances was provided by the regimental Pipes and Drums but other instruments were also played by musicians employed by the regiments. In 1802 the 'Cloathing Account' of the Argyll and Sutherland Highlanders paid out £12 4s 7d (£12.23) for French horns – a favourite instrument in the country-dance bands of that era. The Pipes and Drums of a regiment were, and still are, paid for by officers' subscription, and so one assumes that other instrumentalists were paid by the same means. Reels and country dancing have always been a feature of Scottish regimental leisure and today at least half of a programme for a regimental ball will be given over to them.

In Assembly minutes and newspaper accounts of the early 19th century, reference is frequently made to the presence at balls of officers of regiments stationed locally.

Dancing, too, was a feature of the activity of regimental recruiting sergeants in attendance at country fairs and feeing markets, whose tactics are well recorded in the old song Twa Recruitin' Sergeants. A dancer in full regimental rig was bound to attract a crowd and the more spectacular his performance the better the crowd. Through the throng of watchers would go the recruiters offering the King's shilling to many a country lad naïve enough to imagine that army life must be something to dance about.

The character step dance Wilt Thou Go To The Barracks, Johnnie? originated in the early part of the 19th century and portrays a dancing recruiter with nimble, eye-catching steps.

Like the regiments of Scotland, Scotland's landowners were a peripatetic crowd, spending some part of the year on their estates when they might entertain themselves in style by attending the annual Northern Meeting at Inverness for a week of socializing and general junketing. Other parts of the year might be spent in Edinburgh, or in visiting London which they were doing more and more often.

Edinburgh, however, in the first part of the century, was still the Mecca and in the spacious new houses of the New Town, entertaining at home was very fashionable.

Elizabeth Grant reports that in 1816 'there were very few large balls given this winter. A much more pleasant style of smaller parties had come into fashion with the new style of dancing. It was the first season of the quadrilles against the introduction of which there had been a great stand made by old-fashioned respectables. Many resisted the new French figures altogether, and it was a pity to give up the merry country dance.'

The 'old-fashioned respectables' had good grounds for their resistance. The waltz and the quadrille had already swept the country dances out of the ballrooms of London and the capitals of Europe, and the Scottish elders were understandably strong in their defence of the dance traditions of their youth.

Already, long since, the minuets had been abandoned in the ballrooms with, many considered, a resultant lowering of all standards from moral to motor. No one cared to remember, it seemed, that the minuet had never been particularly popular nor particularly elegant in its Scottish days.

Mrs Home Scott, a Dundee lady born in 1790, recalled in later life a public performance of the minuet.

'I never saw but one minuet danced, or rather walked, in a ballroom. It was the custom for the gentleman who was to take part in this exhibition to secure the honour of the lady's hand several days before the dance took place. On the occasion to which I refer the ball was opened by a single couple minuet, and I distinctly recollect the dress and appearance of the lady and the gentleman.

'The gentleman, who had white, powdered hair, was dressed in a green coat with clear buttons, pale silk knee breeches with silver buckles at the knees, flesh coloured silk stockings, shoes with silver buckles and a large cocked hat.

'The lady, also with powdered hair, was attired in rich brocaded silk, and carried a very large fan.

'The gentleman led out his lady partner with great ceremony, and after making a profound bow to her, which she returned with an equally low curtsey, the minuet was commenced. The exhibition was pleasing, but unexciting. The company of spectators present sat mutely admiring the elegant attitudes and movements of the couple, who, at the close of the performance, retired to a seat, amidst a gentle hum of applause.'

Although that was Mrs Home Scott's only recollection of a minuet in a public ballroom she does record having been at a private ball where she took part in seven minuets in an evening – which is more likely evidence of a dancing master's influence than of real enthusiasm for the dance.

However, the dancing masters with an eye to business had little option but to follow the quadrille fashion, as Elizabeth Grant records.

'We young people were all bit by the quadrille mania, and I was one of a set that brought them first into notice. We practised privately with the aid of a very much better master than Mr. Smart. Finlay Dunn had been abroad, and imported all the most graceful steps from Paris; and having kept our secret well, we burst upon the world at a select reunion at the White Melvilles, the spectators standing on chairs and sofas to admire us.'

Whereas reels and country dances required the participants to stand in lines, in the quadrille the four couples taking part formed a square and in that formation performed a succession of complete dance progressions each with a title. The dancing masters soon were busy learning and introducing new formations and attending to their pupils' footwork.

Elizabeth Grant tells us, 'people *danced* in those days; we did not merely stand and talk, look about bewildered for our vis-à-vis, return to our partners either too soon or too late, without any regard to the completion of the figure, the conclusion of the measure, or the step belonging to it; we attended to our business, we moved in cadence, easily and quietly, embarrassing no one and appearing to advantage ourselves. So well did we all perform, that our exhibition was called for and repeated several times in the course of the evening. We had no trouble in enlisting co-operators, the rage for quadrilles spread, the dancing master was in every house, and every other style discarded.'

It is evident that by the time Elizabeth Grant set down her memoirs, in 1845, the dance had already begun to be less danced than moved through.

James Neill, the renowned Forfar dancing master, recalled in 1908 that in his early teaching days, in the 1850s, the quadrille was still being taught with neat 'French' steps and the teaching of it was a matter of ten lessons and more. But faster music, introduced mid-century, allowed the less schooled dancer to dispense with many of the steps and in time the dancies were expected to teach the quadrille in a couple of lessons.

The introduction of the quadrille in the Edinburgh season of 1816–17 had significant effect on the social life of the day.

According to Elizabeth Grant: 'Room being required for the display much smaller parties were invited. Two, or at most three, instruments sufficed for band, refreshments suited better than suppers, an economy that enabled the inviters to give three or four of these sociable little dances at less cost than one ball.'

Such private, sociable little dances were soon popular with everyone who had room enough for a set of quadrilles. In 1839 Henry Cockburn, now a circuit judge and eminent Law Lord, with his George Square Assembly days far behind him, tells how he enjoyed 'a quadrille party and a solid supper' at the Provost of Aberdeen's house. Quadrille parties became the social order of the day in Scotland for the remainder of the century.

Although quadrille fever had altered the nature of home entertaining, reels and the more popular country dances stood secure in the repertoire of ballroom and assembly room, and in 1822 there occurred an event which almost certainly contributed towards their preservation for posterity. In that year George IV came to his northern capital on a visit stage-managed by Walter Scott, the great romantic.

Edinburgh filled with Highlanders and their chiefs exotically rigged in newly created tartans. The King himself – of rather more than portly dimensions – appeared swathed in kilt and plaid, delighting the ladies one of whom silenced critics of the fat Hanoverian sporting the kilt by declaring that since his stay was to be so short – 'the more we see of him the better!'

The visit was a fantastic success and in a gruelling succession of banquets, parades, displays and balls, Sir Walter – knighted for his pains – succeeded beyond even his own imaginings in rekindling a waning enthusiasm in the Scots not just for their monarch but for their own past. To this day it is claimed that it was then that Scotland's true heritage began to degenerate into tartan-wrapped romanticism and plain sentimentality. Be that as it may, there is no disputing the genuine revival of interest at that time in Scottish traditions, not least in dancing.

Elizabeth Grant was unable to be in Edinburgh for the event, but her sisters, Jane and Mary, wrote her a series of letters which are like a running commentary on all that went on. They reported that at the two great balls given in the king's honour in the George Street Assembly Rooms, 'no part of the entertainment amused his majesty more than the reels for which he stood upwards of half an hour to observe'. The sight of the king in tartan watching his loyal subjects execute their ancient traditional dance must have provided a curious balm for the Scots who were at that period experiencing tremendous turmoil in their society.

Lowland Scotland, when the New Town of Edinburgh was

in its early stages of building, was still basically an agricultural society made up of a literate rural population led by hereditary landowners, and both classes had long lived cheek-by-jowl. Between the two had grown up a trading middle class and the three groups rubbed along together, each well aware of their own worth and place in society. But since 1780 all that had been changing, and changing fast.

Enclosures and improvements on Lowland estates revolutionized land management. Villages, which had not hitherto been a feature of the Scottish landscape, grew up or were created by lairds as settlements for folk who, in the regrouping and redrawing of farm boundaries, were persuaded, or forced, to give up their tenanted few acres.

For the first time in rural Scotland, communities existed where it was possible to live independent of the laird. And in urban Scotland, industrialization was in the process of depersonalizing the age-old relationship between man and master.

In such an atmosphere of often unsympathetic change, folk clung to habits and ways which recalled for them more leisured, less unsettled times. As the century progressed, the population increased dramatically, polarizing into rural or urban communities as remote from each other in life-style as if they had been on two different planets.

Yet thanks to the activities of the dancing masters, there was a common bond in dancing. The middle and upper working classes in the towns and cities learned their quadrilles, mazurkas, waltzes, and the like in dance studios and public halls. The country youth would gather in a farm kitchen, a schoolroom or a barn, or, in some instances, they would share their lessons with the laird's family at the 'big hoose'.

When Queen Victoria paid her first visit to Scotland in 1842 she was greeted off St Abb's head by a large steamer on which people danced a reel to the music of a band . . . the first of many reels danced for Her Majesty in the Balmoral years to come.

When she and Prince Albert made their first foray into Perthshire, she recorded in her journal that she was entertained at Dunkeld when 'one of the Highlanders danced the "sword dance" (Two swords laid upon the ground, and the dancer has to dance across them without touching them.) Some of the others danced a reel.'

Wherever the royal couple travelled on that first visit they were treated to displays of reels. At a ball at Taymouth Castle, although the evening began with the ninety guests joining in a quadrille, 'a number of reels were danced, which it was very amusing and pretty to see'.

After several visits to her northern kingdom, in 1855 the

Queen and Prince Consort first occupied the newly rebuilt Balmoral Castle, and almost every subsequent event of note there had its accompaniment of piping and dancing.

The royal style of Highland life – the pony treks, the organized shooting, the picnics and the dancing of an evening – was the model imitated by scores of southerners; the titled, the nouveau riche manufacturers of England's Midlands, the merchant millionaires of London, who now came north in droves each year to magnificent new shooting lodges and summer homes which sprang up all over the eastern Highlands.

There is no doubt that those incomers, the new tenants and lairds with their southern tongues, imposed their own ideas of Scottishness on their surroundings. Their houses were marvellous affairs, all turreted and crow-stepped in 'Scottish Baronial' massiveness. And in their enthusiasm for things Highland they adopted, when they came north, what they supposed to be Scottish dress and Scottish ways, often sorely trying native self-control in face of the downright ridiculous.

Accustomed as they were in England to a servant class which was, above all, subservient, they often considered the native Scots impertinent, stubborn and intractable. The 17th-century English rural social mix, observed by M. de Muralt, was something long lost. And the English did not understand the time-honoured laird-man relationship which had been mutually respectful. Not for them the likes of the Duchess of Gordon's parties, described by Elizabeth Grant, where the servant lasses and the herd lads danced with, and often better than, the lords and ladies.

Yet it must have impressed many of the incomers, when they dropped in at a servants' or a ghillies' ball, that the dances being enjoyed were more or less identical to those they danced themselves, and the reels and 'quaint' country dances were being performed in a manner which they envied and admired. That this was so was almost entirely due to the activities of the rural dancies, who had been busy in the countryside for over two hundred years.

In a remote place a dancie might be a gifted amateur who pursued another profession by day and taught dancing to his neighbours' children simply as a pastime. The vast majority of dancies, however, were men who made their living entirely from their activities as teachers of dancing and perhaps a musical instrument or two. And by the time Robert Burns went to a dancie's classes in Tarbolton in 1779, against his father's will, the touring masters were a very familiar part of Scotland's social scene.

Even if the children of Lord and Lady Thisandthat attended

the classes of an Edinburgh master when they were in town, their basic lessons in dancing were more often than not received from an itinerant master either in their homes or at the public session at the parish school, where they also received their basic education. Thus the flowers of Edinburgh society might well have had their first lessons in deportment and the minuet from a dancie. The contribution made by dancies to the country's social life was immeasurable.

Normally a dancie organized his work from his home, although, in a larger burgh, he might have a dancing studio which would also be the office where he planned his year's work. In a country where dancing had long been considered part of a polite education, he rarely had much difficulty in gathering classes together at different venues throughout the countryside.

Permission might be sought to hold lessons in a schoolroom after school hours or classes might be held in a farm kitchen or a barn. In order to drum up trade, the dancie might put on a small concert or demonstration 'assembly', bringing pupils with him from other centres to demonstrate the High dances and country dancing, callisthenics, deportment exercises, and the like. He would also advertise his projected session of lessons in the local press.

Then, when a class had been gathered together, weekly lessons were held at the appointed centre. Usually, the very young were taught just after school closing time, the older children and adults having their classes later in the same evening.

In all centres, town and country alike, the session of lessons always ended in a finishing assembly which served to show off to admiring elders what had been achieved, and to let them see they'd got their money's worth.

There were parents who had decided views on allowing their offspring to take part in these public displays, although such an attitude seems to have been more prevalent among the middle classes in the towns than in the countryside.

Mary I. Ogilvie, whose book *A Scottish Childhood* is a record of growing up in Dundee, tells how, in 1865, her formal education began at a girls' school where a drill sergeant-cum-dancing master gave lessons.

'No objection was made by my parents to my learning dancing at school. I was not permitted, however, to figure in the Display in a public hall at the end of term. It was always referred to as "The Ball" – a name I suppose which savoured too much of this world. I quite see that in the unlikely event of my being called on to perform a pas seul in the presence of my fellow pupils and their parents, I might have been puffed up with sinful pride, but

I cannot understand how my immortal soul could have been imperilled by joining in a composite dance like the "Wreath Dance" in which I longed to take part.'

To attract new pupils, dancies frequently offered reductions for numbers – a consideration in a society where large families were the order of the day. Often a family with two or more attending classes had the younger fry taught at much reduced rates – sometimes for nothing.

This system persisted into the present century. Dancie Norman Guild in Angus at the beginning of this century was offering a free series of lessons for one child if two in the family were already being paid for.

To present a good assembly was the aim of every dancie and if he could teach a musical instrument as well as dancing, then he could present an impressively varied programme. Add to that the cachet of giving private classes at the 'big hoose' and his reputation was made. What was good enough for the laird's bairns would do fine for the farmer's!

Dancie McLagan of Dundee, who taught in the city from around 1814 to the 1840s, was typical of his profession at that time. He taught his city pupils in the Caledonian Hall in Dundee's Castle Street and later in a Masonic Lodge in the Murraygate, advertising regularly his intention 'to teach, in the most approved manner Minuets, Mazourkas, Gallopades, Cracoviacs etc; with his usual Exercises for improving the ear; as also, a number of elementary Exercises for the improvement of the deportment, as taught by the most fashionable masters in Edinburgh and London'.

Mr McLagan was an ardent improver! A cossack dance which turns up in his finishing assembly programmes is advertised as 'improving the Ear, and use of arms'. His Dance Academy in Dundee was open every evening from five until nine o'clock for 'Country and Figure Dances'. But in the summer with its long light days, Mr McLagan ventured out of town and into the burghs and larger villages of the surrounding countryside, where he also held classes and regular assemblies.

The programme for one of these, his tenth ball at Coupar Angus in Perthshire on 8 July 1824, heralds a dancing display containing no fewer than fifty-six items with an interval of fifteen minutes allowed for refreshment at the end of the first twenty-four. A test of endurance for participants and audience alike. Since the second part of the programme contained several items repeated from the first, it would seem that during the evening every single pupil, from the smallest and least experienced to dancers of considerable ability, had the chance to shine in turn.

Among the items on the programme, which included the Minuet de la Cour, the King of Sweden's March, the Waltz, Quadrille le Lanciers (The Lancers), Quadrille le Garçon Vollage, the Highland Fling, Jackie Tar, and the Spanish Guaracha, is mentioned Reels of Eight. Most likely Mr McLagan's Reels of Eight was an arrangement of foursomes for two sets and not related to the Eightsome Reel which was devised later in the century. Curiously, the evening ends not with a reel, nor with a quadrille, but with a display of 'Shantrush' – Seann Trubhais.

With an eye ever open to future business, Mr McLagan heads his programme for the assembly with an advertising jingle:

> Some will not dance because they canna;
> Others, for different reasons, manna;
> But why not try it, all that's willing?
> Since there is no sin in spilling.

and closes it by bringing to public attention that 'he annually visits his friends in Edinburgh, on their return from Paris; so gets acquainted with the newest and most fashionable styles of Dancing. Mr. McL begs to intimate, that he will continue his usual round in the Summer season; beginning at Cupar Angus, about the 1st May.'

In that same programme it is also announced that the 'celebrated Mr. Archibald Allan is to play the violin', whether Mr Allan played for the accompaniment of dancers or performed solo work isn't stated. It is likely that Mr McLagan was himself a musician and there were, indeed, some renowned musicians among the dancies, many of whom accompanied their dancing lessons on their own fiddles. And a considerable number of them could have made music their entire profession.

Among them were men who composed some very fine music – men such as James Scott Skinner whose name is now almost exclusively associated with his style of fiddle playing and his compositions. He was, for many years, an itinerant dancing master in the north east of Scotland.

Scott Skinner was a dancie whose name was destined to endure through his music – but there was a host of other men of his craft, whose sole memorials now lie in files of old newspaper reports of their assemblies and their pupils' successes, or live in the childhood memories of former pupils.

Dancie Carnegie of the Mearns, Billy Primrose of Paisley, 'Professor' Buck of the Borders, the Adamsons, father and son, from Fife, Dancie Presley and the Cruikshanks from Peterhead, Dancie Dargie from Perth and Dancie Whyte of New Pitsligo who was a postman – an ideal job when it came to searching out prospective pupils! A handful of men from a legion.

In the counties of Angus and Perthshire dancies abounded – dancies who were also musicians of note, and it is not accidental that this part of the country is today in the forefront of the revival of traditional fiddle music. The standards set in the past by teachers of dancing and fiddle music such as John Reid of Newtyle and his teacher James Neill of Forfar, still persist. The latter was, and is still remembered as, the doyen of dancies and fiddlers in the Angus and Perthshire of his day.

His career as a teacher began in 1855 and continued until 1918 when he was eighty-four. James Neill received – in fact, earnestly went in search of – a more formal training in dancing and music than many dancies.

He was born on the Glamis Estate, near Forfar, into a musical family who attempted oddly enough to discourage his interest in learning to play the fiddle. But it seems that when the boy would be put off no longer, he received full parental backing and had both fiddle and dancing lessons from the Lowe brothers of Perth.

In due course James Neill settled in Forfar and began his life-long work as a teacher of dancing and music. He soon became known as a first-rate teacher, not just by the country folk who flocked to his classes in Strathmore and in the foothills of the Angus glens, but also by the gentry in the great houses and castles which abound in the area.

From letters in the possession today of his grandson, it can be learned that Dancie Neill was expected not only to teach dancing but also to supply orchestras and bands for this servants' ball and that children's party, this Harvest Home, and that Grand Ball. As a purveyor of music and musicians, he became an institution in his lifetime.

Carse Grey,
Forfar.

Mr Neill,
Could you come tomorrow any time after
10 o'clock and give a lesson in reels,
as some of our party want a little
brushing up.

Balhary,
Meigle.

Mrs. Denroche-Smith will be glad to know
if Mr. Neill can come here next Tuesday
or Wednesday afternoon and give his old
class a lesson – she supposes the charge
will be 10/6d [52½ pence] as last year.

Faskally,
Pitlochry.
19th Dec. 1907

I am having a servants' dance in Fishers' Hotel here
on 31st December; there will be eighty people or so
there. Can you send a band that night?

Beechwood,
by Dundee.
Dec. 10. '03.

Dear Sir,
    We are giving a children's dance on the 6th January
and I should be glad if you can play for us and get someone
to play the piano and perhaps cornet, and send me a copy of
a programme.
    The children will be aged from 7 years to 17 or 18.
Kindly let me know by return if you are engaged for that
date.

The hours of this dance were from 6.30 to 11.30 and the
programme was altered to include waltzes of which 'the young
gentlemen wished to have as many as possible'. One can but
admire the hostess for wishing to put together five hours of
entertainment for such a disparate age group. But, since the
children involved were mostly pupils of the dancie, the evening
would have been spent happily at the dances he had taught them
– with no age barriers in evidence.
    We know which dances Dancie Neill taught towards the end
of his career from the programmes for his finishing assemblies.
One such programme for an assembly held at Coupar Angus in
1898 contains the following items:

1 Grand Entree of Pupils   2 Quadrille   3 Jack Tar Country
Dance   4 Polka   5 Free Gymnastics, bar bell exercises,
marching drill   6 Scotch steps   7 Highland Schottische
8 Ancient Sword Dance (Ladies)   9 Ancient Sword Dance
(Gentlemen)   10 Valse Minuet   11 Eightsome Reel   12
Quadrille   13 Pas Seul – Ladies Hornpipe [on this occasion
danced by his daughter Griselda]   14 and 15 Highland Fling
for ladies and gentlemen   16 The Guaracha   17 Washington
Post   18 A Medley of French, Scotch and Irish steps   19 A New
Dance – 'Royal Record'   20 Cotillion   21 Waltz   22 Pas de
deux   23 Berlin Polka   24 The Lancers   25 Reel O' Tulloch
and Foursome.   The Finale was a polka.

Mr Neill always took care to announce in his programme the
date of the start of the next session of lessons, and one can
imagine the non-dancers among the children in the audience

clamouring to be allowed to learn and have their chance to show off their paces at future assemblies.

Of course, showing off was sternly discouraged. James Neill was a stickler for the correct way of doing things, and not just the correct, but the traditional. At his finishing balls even in the smallest, least populous centres, the reels would be danced by four boys or youths to bagpipe music if at all possible.

This attention to tradition led him inevitably into confrontation with those who attempted to modernize Scottish music. On one occasion, for instance, he was asked by the Duchess of Atholl to supply band parts for Scottish dancing to a German band fashionable at the time and hired by Her Grace to supply the music for a ball at Blair Castle.

James Neill's orchestra had long been in the habit of providing the music at Blair Castle and it certainly wasn't particularly tactful of the Duchess to make such a request of him. However, she was very quickly put straight on the matter by the redoubtable dancie whose notes for his reply were found scribbled on the back of one of his assembly programmes.

'There is no use in writing . . . [indecipherable] for reel time, they were never meant for this and no one knows better than Herr —— if he wants to play some reels he can do so from the [indecipherable] quite well. The violins and flute can easily play from the piano part, the basses also, and the cornets can extemporise a part. That is all that is required.

'But they cannot play reels. At any rate, they can play the reels, but they don't give them the Scotch snap and proper accent for dancing. They may as well try to speak Gaelic.

'The fact is they don't think they are worth playing. They just burlesque them. But if I have the honour of playing at Blair Castle —' and there the notes end.

He sent this reply, or something like it, since he played at the castle soon after and often in following years, and we hear no more of German bands at Blair Atholl!

James Neill was a well-known and favourite figure among the aristocracy of his day. In 1908 he was presented with one hundred guineas and a large silver trophy by his 'county' pupils among whom at that time was one Lady Elizabeth Bowes-Lyon – the Queen Mother.

Also learning her dancing at Glamis at the time, but in the Masonic Hall in the village, was the lady who sent the author the following account of her dancing days.

'I was almost five when I had my first quarter, and my first teacher was Dancie Neill from Forfar. He cycled the six miles to Glamis once a week with his fiddle on his back. I remember he taught us the Highland Fling and also the sword dance and he had a class of between 30 and 40. He also taught us the Lancers and the Quadrilles and we got a maypole dance when we had to go in two round the pole and pleat the ribbons. It was very pretty. But the highlight of it all was the Finishing Ball where we all got dressed up in lovely dresses and big bows of ribbon in our hair and sashes to match our dresses and all took part in the Grand March.

'I shall always remember it. The boys were not allowed to dash across the floor to grab a partner. They had to walk over, bow and say, "May I have the pleasure?" There was a boy the same age and size as I was and Mr Neill always made him dance as my partner and everybody called him my boyfriend and thought it was great fun except me.'

Another former pupil remembered how a none too gentle tap with the fiddle bow would straighten a back or correct a badly-placed leg. But Dancie Neill was a good teacher who firmly believed in varying his lessons and keeping the attention and interest of the children alive.

He knew that he got his pupils at the end of a day's schooling when they were a mixture of weariness and pent-up energy. He knew the dancing classes were as much a matter of letting off steam as of learning, and he believed that country dancing and reels were the perfect means of doing both. Hence he never neglected to teach country dances along with the 'High' and step dances of the day, as his programmes show.

'There is only a certain time that we can secure the attention of children,' he wrote, 'after that you may punish them, but this will not be progress. Good results are produced not by long hours but by method.' He had method and he also had good music. His pupils learned their dancing to music in the finest tradition. The music he used to accompany his teaching is still in the possession of his family. There are fine volumes of late 18th-century and early 19th-century collections of dance music and a variety of folders of James Neill's own transcriptions and orchestrations of dance tunes and concert pieces.

Apart from his dance teaching he also taught violin, viola and cello and his pupils gave regular concerts of solo and orchestral music of non-Scottish origin. His pupils' concerts were as much a highlight of the social year as his finishing balls.

There are many similarities between Francis Peacock at the beginning of the 19th century and James Neill at its end. Both strove to maintain high standards in changing times. Peacock feared the effects of the passing of the minuet, James Neill bemoaned a lack of interest in the *steps* of popular country dances and reels.

But by the end of the century there was hardly a child in the

Lowland countryside who wasn't having at least a lesson or two in dancing and the repertoire of social dances generally taught in the countryside was a mixture of old country dances, reels, quadrilles and lancers, couple dances such as the Highland Schottische, the Gay Gordons, La Varsoviana Waltz – La Va for short – and the waltz and the polka. There were also the round-the-room dances such as The Dashing White Sergeant and the Waltz Country Dance.

The country dances which had remained popular throughout the century included Petronella, The Flo'ers of Edinburgh, The Duke of Perth, Strip the Willow, Haymakers. Add to these the country dances being created and taught by dancies throughout the countryside, and the total of dances known to Scotland's rural population in the 19th century was considerable.

The old reels, of course, never fell from grace. Threesomes and Foursomes were always danced and when, in the 1870s, a dance was devised which was a mixture of the old ring dance and Threesomes, called an Eightsome Reel, it was an immediate success and became lastingly popular.

Another genre of dances which had gained popularity in the 19th century were the so-called Swedish dances which involved couples facing each other and passing on at the end of each complete dance sequence to confront a new couple – and so on, round the room. Among these dances was one which makes its initial appearance in Dundee dancing master David Anderson's *Universal Ballroom and Solo Dance Guide* of 1890, under the title La Danse Florence – a mix of Threesomes and 'Swedish'.

In 1826 a song, The Dashing White Sergeant, had been published and the tune, by Sir Henry Bishop, soon passed into the repertoire of dance bands. It wasn't until almost the end of the century that The Dashing White Sergeant tune met up with La Danse Florence to give us the combination which remains today one of the most popular of dances.

The Waltz Country Dance, combining waltz steps and music with the 'Swedish' progression, brought into the dance musicians' repertoire a great wealth of Scottish song tunes in waltz time.

By the end of the 19th century there was a very marked gulf between the dances being taught in the cities and towns and those the dancies were teaching in the countryside. The forces of fashion being much stronger in urban society, the teacher there, in order to survive professionally, had to keep abreast of – or ahead of – the dance vogue of the moment. Consequently in the towns the country dances were neglected.

A. Cosmo Mitchell, a notable Aberdeen dancing teacher from 1881 until the mid 1920s – and as 'official' as Peacock had been since Mitchell was eventually appointed dancing master to the city's public schools – held regular dancing exhibitions with programmes containing not a single country dance of the longways type.

A typical programme of his was the one for a dancing exhibition in Ferryhill Public School in March 1893. The items were as follows:

1 Waltz   2 Scotch Reel   3 Waltz Country Dance   4 Quadrille
5 Polka   6 Lancers   7 Circassian Circle   8 German Schottische
9 Waltz   10 Lancers   11 Waltz Minuet   12 Polka
13 Pas de Quatre   14 Waltz Cotillon   15 Highland Schottische

A. Cosmo Mitchell also taught the 'High' and character dances – Seann Trubhais, the Sword Dance, Highland Fling, the Irish Jig – but more regularly his exhibitions are given over to items with titles such as Tantivy, La Galligada, Parisian Polka, the Washington Post, Scarborough Gavotte and, later, the Aeroplane Waltz and the Motor Polka. 'German' dances such as the Gavotte des Kaiserin and the German Schottische make their last appearance in his dance programmes of 1914.

Contrast these contents with a Dancie Neill rural class programme of the same era containing Scotch Reels, Petronella, Jack Tar, The Haymakers, The Duke of Perth, and several items marked simply Country Dance with title unspecified, and we have considerable evidence that had it not been for the earnest work and enthusiasm of the rural dancies, by the end of the century many of the old country dances would have been in danger of being lost altogether.

But just as a few city teachers did retain some country dances in their repertoire, so the country dancie had to bow a little before the fashion for 'modern' dancing. In 1898 Dancie Neill was schooling his pupils in the Washington Post which had become a popular twosome in city ballrooms. A newspaper reported the Forfar première of the dance.

'Mr. Neill, who is in the front rank of his profession, has, this season, introduced several new dances, the most notable among them being the much-talked-of "Washington Post". It is essentially a dance of youth – a terpsichorean novelty; and as the bewitching young ladies charmingly tripped it to the popular march tune, the toes of the grown-ups must have itched to join in the game. "The Post" is an American curiosity and bids fair to rival the quaint barn dance. It is a departure from the usual order of affairs, inasmuch as the gentleman stands behind the lady, and holds her hands over her head, dancing with a kind of chassez step, the pose showing off a fine figure to perfection. The "Washington Post" dance seems to have broken down the old barriers of ballroom formality, and has animated many of the recent functions.'

In fact, the 'old barriers of ballroom formality' had long gone. Couples now waltzed and polka-ed in a manner of informality and physical intimacy undreamed of when the century began. The Washington Post was only one of several American curiosities which were the front-runners, the vanguard, of what was to become an American invasion of influences and styles – a seemingly irresistible force in the twentieth century.

6

ELEGANTLY, FOR MISS MILLIGAN

In the 19th-century ballrooms of Europe the country dances had been replaced by the waltz, the quadrille and the polka. And, despite the growing trend towards nationalism in European music, this development did not extend to social dancing apart from the invention of a few mock-traditional ballroom couple dances based on ancient national dances such as the mazurka and the cracoviac in Poland. In Scotland, although such foreign dances were part of the dancing masters' repertoire, the old social dances, the country dances and reels, remained and, instead of being replaced, were simply augmented by new types of Scottish ballroom dance. Waltz steps and quadrille formations found themselves blended with older native dances and the result was a singularly happy marriage of styles.

At the end of the 19th century, although ragtime and early jazz were beginning to catch on in other places, the initial impact on Scotland was not great. By the end of the first decade of the century, however, in the towns and cities, the old dances were already out of favour and in a considerable state of neglect and, when jazz did get properly underway in these places, the American dances simply replaced last year's fashionable 'Parisian' waltz or 'German' polka.

But in the countryside the old dances continued to be taught and danced and we have an excellent account of social dancing in the years before the First World War in Lewis Grassic Gibbon's *Sunset Song* – the first book of his trilogy, *A Scots Quair*.

In *Sunset Song*, Chris Guthrie, the heroine, marries and her wedding dance, held in the barn of the farm of Blawearie, typifies the dancing in the countryside, which the author would have witnessed as a child in Kincardine.

At Chris's wedding there are two instruments to provide the music, the accordion and the fiddle, and the dances described are Eightsomes, Petronella, Strip The Willow, schottisches and waltzes. The scene at Blawearie would have been a familiar one to Scottish country dwellers in the years before the Great War.

For a number of years which were to prove vital in the story of Scottish dancing, the country folk continued to resist

American influences and it was not until the years following the First World War that that resistance was finally breached.
In the war the familiar world collapsed. Broken down and dismissed forever were many of the Victorian social strictures, the old ideals, and the survivors of the holocaust set off in serious pursuit of novelty and modernity at any price.

At the war's end the traditional dances, even in the countryside, lost ground rapidly to the new styles and sounds from the other side of the Atlantic. The dancies did not abandon the teaching of the step and country dances altogether but, by the 1920s, advertisements for dancing classes in country places now offered tuition in the one-step, the two-step, foxtrot, quickstep, tango and the Jazz Twinkle, and there was no adapting of these steps and dances to the native Scottish style, nor any hope of absorption and the emergence of Scottish native jazz!

The changes were not just musical and terpsichorean, they were also sociological. Whereas in the past the Scots had been in the habit of dancing in sociable sets, now they indulged in what one rueful observer described as 'commercialised recreation for exclusive couples'.

All was not lost, though. For a considerable time there had been concern in the cities about the disappearance of the old dances from circulation. Even before the Great War there had existed in Glasgow a group, called the Beltane Society, who met in private houses to learn old country dances, the chief teacher of which was a lecturer at Jordanhill College of Education, Miss Jean Milligan.

Miss Milligan's interest in the old social dances had begun when she was a very little girl. Although her family had long lived in Glasgow, where she grew up, her mother had come from Roxburgh in the Borders and had been an enthusiastic dancer in her day. This enthusiasm she passed to her daughter who remembered well the delight she had as a child in being allowed to watch the maid servants and their lads dance in the kitchen of the Milligans' home. Fascinated, she watched huge country-bred members of Glasgow's Police Force trip ballet-like through old reels and country dances; and this early enthralment never left her.

The Beltane Society's activities were halted by the Great War although Miss Milligan's interest did not wane, and, dismayed by the trends in dancing in Scotland after the war, she wondered what could be done to revive interest in the old dances and their music.

Even during her Beltane Society days, Miss Milligan had been aware of how difficult it was to be sure of the old ways. What *were* the old dances? Where did one find them? Few books of dance instruction were in existence. Dances with the same title but with different figures existed in various parts of the country because of the habit of taking the title of a dance from the tune to which it was danced. And by the same token, one set of figures making up a dance could be known by three different titles – for instance, the Duke of Perth was also called Broun's Reel and Clean Pease Strae depending upon which part of the country it was being danced in.

And there was also the matter of steps and progressions. A poussette might be danced in half a dozen different ways depending upon the dancies' willingness to allow the waltz hold and step, or the elbow grip, or linked arms, and the like.

There was, then, little literature, no uniformity, no standards to judge or progress by, and, above all, before long there would be no one left to remember so many of the old dances long since left out of programmes.

Sadly, it seemed to Miss Milligan, there would soon be nothing more inspiring than a rough-house Eightsome left as a memorial to Scottish dancing's elegant Golden Age.

That this did not happen is almost entirely due to the energy and exertions of Jean Milligan who, with Mrs Ysabel Stewart of Fasnacloich, founded the Scottish Country Dance Society in 1923. With the backing of a promise of £300 from Paterson's, the Glasgow music publishers, the two ladies called a public meeting of all interested at Glasgow's Athenaeum in that year and were overwhelmed by the throng which turned up in response to their invitation.

There and then the Society was formed with Brigadier-General Cheape as the first President, a position taken up the following year by Lord James Stewart-Murray, later Duke of Atholl. Lord James, who had learned his dancing from Dancie Neill, remained President until his death in 1957.

At the opening meeting of the Society it was decided that the publication of a book of dances be proceeded with immediately, and this task was undertaken by Miss Milligan and Mrs Stewart. This first book was to contain twelve dances in all – six from Miss Milligan and six from Mrs Stewart – and it was now that the vital years of rural resistance to American dances bore fruit. There still were older people throughout the land who remembered the dances they had been taught in childhood, dances taught by the dancies in barns and village halls. And there were still dancies only too willing to give account of the dances they had been taught and were teaching.

The work of collecting and reviving was begun – not, however, to unanimous plaudits and encouragement. The opinion was prevalent that Miss Milligan and Mrs Stewart would gather enough material for two books, possibly three. But Miss Milligan's determination to reintroduce the old social dances into Scotland's ballrooms was greeted with considerable scorn. It was sincerely felt that it would be possible, indeed praiseworthy, to teach the country dances to 'captive' groups such as Girl Guides, Boy Scouts, Boys' Brigade, Women's Rural Institutes and in schools, but unrealistic to believe that the dances would ever find general favour again.

Miss Milligan in particular was accused of being unrealistic in attempting to restore a Golden Age – to revive the ways of two centuries back was to ignore intervening evolution and revolution. But it never was Miss Milligan's aim, or the purpose of the Society, to restore former times, the aim was simply to find a historical foundation for the Society's work and development.

Miss Milligan, in those early years, might merely have made some historical notes and printed some dances, leaving posterity with a record of what people recalled but rarely danced in the year 1923. This would have served posterity well enough as the record of an era but would have ignored completely the contribution of previous centuries to the evolution of the dances and dancing styles, and, at a time when fast-changing fashion had almost obliterated the folk memory of old social dances, this would have been almost criminal. One may imagine the judgement of history on Jean Milligan had she shut her mind to what she suspected was a glorious past and concentrated merely on preserving what people remembered from the recent past.

The decision having been made to search for dances in manuscripts and old books, the problem arose of the actual suitability of the name of the Society. Country dances were, strictly speaking, the longways dances which had first become popular in the 17th century. What had commonly come to be called country dances in Scotland were, in fact, a variety of social dances, old reels, country dances, round-the-room couple dances and quadrille-type dances. It was agreed, however, since the term 'country dance' *had* come to be applied to all these forms of ballroom dance, that the title Scottish Country Dance Society would suit the Society's purpose. But settling on the Society's name was a minor problem in those infant days. Far greater were the decisions which must be made about the revival and style of the dances themselves. How were they to be performed?

Was it correct to dance a dance of 1757 or even of 1857 in the nondescript style of 1923? And since that style in 1923 in Angus differed considerably from that in Ayrshire, which style was to be applied to a dance created in Aberdeenshire or Fife a century and more before?

Not everyone approved the answer Miss Milligan and the Society found, which was to standardize the steps and figures. Those who disapproved accused Miss Milligan of ignoring the fact that the development of steps and figures was a continuing process and to standardize them would mean that dance evolution would be halted. Such protest ignored the plain fact that the once elegant steps and figures had 'evolved' almost out of existence. A revival of steps and the proper execution of the figures was crucial to the revival of the dances.

By dint of diligent research and her own flair for the dance, Miss Milligan succeeded in standardizing reel and strathspey travelling steps, setting steps and the slip-step which the society accepted along with the old pas de Basque. For authority for her steps Miss Milligan referred to Peacock's 'Sketches' and to later Scottish teachers. Earlier authorities on choreography in France and England were also consulted since it was evident that country dancing masters in Scotland in the 18th century had been influenced by these, and the smooth, gliding steps of modern country dances were constructed.

Figures such as the poussette and the allemande posed problems, too. The former, for instance, had by the 20th century degenerated into a waltz around and partners were linked as for the waltz, which would have been quite unthinkable when the poussette was first introduced. An alternative name for the poussette at the time of its creation was the 'draw' which did suggest the joining of hands for the figure, and Mrs Stewart and Miss Milligan, acting upon corroborating information they had received from an elderly lady, proposed that the Society adopt the two-handed poussette.

There were howls of protest from all over the country. Where, demanded the protesters, had the Society got their authority for the handhold poussette? No one in living memory, surely, had performed it thus!

Apart from the old lady's memories, all the authority required turned up in letters known as the Blantyre Manuscript. A dancing master called A. Smith writing to William Watson of Blantyre Farm in 1802 wrote, 'When you Poussette you take your partner by both hands, the 2cu [second couple] the same, and then move round one another, some times ending where you began and some times in 2cu place as it may answer the musick or according to what may follow.'

The poussette handhold adopted by the society ran into a further problem in that the figure still had the waltzing footwork.

For the sake of neatness and elegance Miss Milligan established the 'four-square' figure used today with the rhyme which rings in the ears of all who learned their country dancing from a Miss Milligan-trained teacher:

> *Away from the centre, turn,*
> *Up or down, turn,*
> *Into the centre, turn round,*
> *Fall back, fall back.*

Firmly resolved not to invent movements to the old figures, and always to have authority of some sort for the revival of figures and steps, Miss Milligan and Mrs Stewart were forced to leave several old dances which had been culled from dance instruction books 'on the table' since they could not properly interpret the instructions.

Early in her work Miss Milligan was confronted by the figure instruction 'allemande'. There had been, she knew, early references in Scotland to Almains and Alemans, and the Allemande was a couple dance popular in France in the 18th century – perhaps the figure had derived from that. However, she could find no clue as to how it had been danced in former times and it looked as though the dances with the allemande figure would have to lie 'on the table' permanently.

Then one day at home, she happened to mention the problem to her mother who thereupon rose to her feet, took hold of Miss Milligan's arms in the graceful allemande hold and demonstrated the elegant figure she'd learned in her youth!

During the first eight years of its life, the young Society published seven books of collected dances and made errors in interpretation and in musical choice, which were quickly admitted and corrected. The dances published were either collected at first hand in the countryside or adapted from country-dance instruction books and manuscripts of the previous two centuries. Miss Milligan and Mrs Stewart were now thoroughly aware that they had only begun to scratch the surface of a very rich field.

Very early in those years, the founders adopted a system of training teachers to instruct others in the Society's approved steps and dances, and the missionary work was earnestly begun. Numbered among the earliest qualified instructors were leaders of youth organizations, members of the Scottish Women's Rural Institutes, teachers of dancing and many physical education teachers who had been familiar for some time with country dancing, thanks to Miss Milligan's work at Jordanhill.

Two branches of the Society were formed in the very first

year, in Glasgow and Edinburgh, and soon branches, clubs and classes sprang up all over the country.

By 1932 the Society had an energetic Publications Committee and a Propaganda and Publicity Committee who lost no opportunity in publicizing and furthering the aims of the Society. For instance, in those days when the Royal Highland and Agricultural Society's shows changed venue each year, the Scottish Country Dance Society set up their own display stand at the shows. There they sold their literature and gramophone records, gave demonstrations and spread the word to country folk.

And the Society never missed an opportunity to display the dances. A team of dancers was sent to London to the International Folk Dance Congress, in 1935, and gave a memorable display in the Albert Hall. Another team, the renowned Dancers of Don, in October 1937, travelled to the BBC's television studios at Alexandra Palace in London where they presented the first ever programme of Scottish country dancing on television.

In fact, the BBC was quick to take notice of the activities of the Scottish Country Dance Society, broadcasting from its earliest days programmes of dance music. Mr Herbert Wiseman, who became the Head of Scottish Music at the BBC in Glasgow, in 1946, was for several years an arranger of music for the Society.

In these early radio days the programmes of country dance music, which became such a regular feature of Scottish radio, were a source of considerable vexation to the Society in that the music was very often performed by ensembles and orchestras with little regard for proper instrumentation, tempi or appropriate tunes for the announced dances.

Ian Whyte, the BBC's Head of Music in Scotland at the time, and an eminent conductor and composer, suffered many a knuckle-rap from the Society for the poor quality of Scottish dance music he allowed on his programmes. In time, though, and after several meetings between Mr Whyte and Miss Milligan, standards improved and considerable attempts were made to standardize the pace of dances so that one did not gallop a strathspey nor stroll a reel.

The Society laid down its own rulings on the matter of timing, in 1934, and has campaigned tirelessly since to get all Scottish country dance bands to pay heed to their suggestions. Arriving at their decisions on timing, the Society had to take into account the requirements of the recreated steps, the old dance figures and the opinions of the better country dance band musicians.

Among their number was Dancie John Reid of Newtyle in Angus who was a member of the Society's Publications

Committee for many years. In the early 1920s John Reid, like most other dancies, had been teaching the modern jazz ballroom dancing along with traditional country dances and Highland and step dances. The jazz dances he threw over completely in favour of teaching the Society's revived dances, and he became a very active missionary on their behalf. He was also in demand by the Society as a teacher of Highland and step dances at the Society's summer schools and as the provider of dance music for the schools' finishing assemblies and important balls.

The Society had very quickly got into the way of holding meetings for branch members and enthusiasts in their summer schools which, by the early thirties, were being held regularly at St Andrews.

Such was the Society's progress in these early years of publicity and propaganda that, in its Annual Report of 1933, the feeling was expressed that 'Scottish country dancing has now, in many places, become so much a part of the life of the people that it no longer calls for special nurturing by the Society.'

There was to be no resting on laurels, though, no flagging of the missionary zeal, for a new development in the Society's activities was beginning to show, and, with suitable encouragement, it might bear fruit.

From its inception, interest had been shown in the work of the Society by European folk dancers. More significant still, two young Australian ladies, in Scotland for a time, had earned the Society's teaching certificate and had declared their intention to begin a Scottish Country Dance Society branch in Sydney on their return home. This they did, and soon reports were coming into the Society of like enthusiasts setting up country dance classes round the globe.

Those were Empire days, and whenever two or more Scots gathered together, a Caledonian or St Andrews Society sprang up and flourished, often in the unlikeliest places.

Otago, New Zealand; Vancouver, Canada; Durban, South Africa with their considerable immigrant Scottish populations were natural enough locations for country dance clubs to flourish – but Shanghai, Calcutta, Cairo?

Yet there, too, Scots got together to dance regularly to instructions from the Society's publications, with music scratched out on early Beltona 78 r.p.m. discs. In Shanghai, the dancers were well favoured with a succession of British garrison Highland regiment pipe-majors as instructors and with regimental pipers to provide music for a hundred dancers and more. So popular was Scottish country dancing in Cairo that it was soon adopted as part of the physical education syllabus in all Egyptian schools.

In schools at home country dancing was now regularly taught thanks to the enthusiasm of young gym teachers who had gained the Society's Teachers' Certificates at college. The children, albeit unwittingly, were receiving a first-class grounding in poise and manners, both inherent in the revived dances.

When the country went to war once more in 1939, many feared that the work of the Society would founder as traditional dancing had in the First World War. The work would either be so seriously curtailed as to be worthless, or the dances would pass from public favour under pressure of other influences.

What did happen, in fact, was that Scottish country dancing became almost an official part of the war effort. In Government-sponsored youth centres and clubs all over Britain, Scottish country dancing was part of the approved programme of events, with teachers supplied by the Society. Country dancing was the order of the day for all soldiers in Scottish Command and country dancing was also a vital part of off-duty entertainment.

Mrs Jane Mowat of Wick, a sergeant in the ATS during the war, recalled in a letter her own particular memories of country dancing in wartime Britain.

'I got an overseas posting to Orkney around 1944 (it really was classed as overseas with a free issue of cigarettes, etc.). At one stage one of our officers, Miss Waterson of Edinburgh, offered to teach us country dancing and since few of us had danced since schooldays we took up her offer and many an enjoyable night we had.

'Winters in Orkney were quite something, especially in Nissen huts, and I'm sure we did many dances, but the one that really stands out in my mind is the "Glasgow Highlanders" to the accompaniment of shrieking wind and rattling roof sheets.

'A year or so later, when the prisoners were being released from Germany, we had a unit of Cameron Highlanders who had been prisoners posted to a camp some five or six miles along the road. Their C.O. sent an invitation to our unit asking if any of our girls would be interested in joining the men in country dancing classes. He stressed that his men had been away from female company so long that he wanted only girls who were genuinely interested in dancing and not in flirting with his men! As you may know the ratio was something like 300 men to one woman in Orkney during the war so we really had to be interested in country dancing to pass up all the other entertainment so eagerly set before us!

'Many a night we trundled in an open-backed army lorry along to the Camerons' camp. We were dressed to the nines – as far as we could in uniform which happily included a tartan skirt.

'Our instructor was a Sgt. Watson of the Royal Army Medical Corps and our classes went on for many weeks, probably until the Orkney summer came, since my recollections are all of standing up in the swaying lorry and looking back into the darkness of rain or wind and, at times, moonlight on snow.

'The men were all very good dancers and this mystified us somewhat. Being a good dancer even in tackety boots, was one thing, but to be a good country dancer and a man as well was something new to us, and intriguing.

'In fact they had all learned their country dancing in Prisoner of War camps. At first their music had been whistling or the mouth organ, a chanter or pipe music if they were lucky, and then records were sent to them in Red Cross parcels. As you can appreciate, the men who had been accustomed for years to dance as ladies found it a bit strange to be dancing as men.'

In the early reverses of the Second World War, great numbers of Scottish soldiers had been imprisoned by the Germans, particularly after the disaster at St Valéry when thousands of men of the 51st Highland Division were captured.

Since the regular soldiers of the Scottish regiments had been in the habit of dancing reels and solo Highland dances, what better way to pass the time in camps than to vary their physical exercises with dancing. Soon requests for help began to filter through to the Scottish Country Dance Society via the Red Cross. Miss Milligan, in 1940, received a letter from a soldier who had left his books of country dances in a French ditch on his run for Dunkirk.

In Stalag 383 in Höhenfels, Bavaria, a camp of NCOs who refused to work for the Germans occupied their time learning Highland dancing and country dancing. Everyone was welcome to join in – English, Australians, Cypriots and New Zealanders as well as Scots. The quality of the instruction was of the highest, the Highland dancing being taught by John Mitchellson of Balmoral and Charlie Mitchell of Ayr with pipe music from Corporal Scott of Aberdeen. The country dancing was in the capable hands of Society members Johnnie Williamson and Innes Russell of Perth, but couple dances longways for as many as will, with brawny Scots as 'ladies', bemused German guards who failed to understand the Scots' delight in dancing.

A report in the Scottish Country Dance Society's Bulletin of June 1941 heralded a story which has since become well known in the annals of Scottish country dancing. Mrs Harris Hunter, Secretary of the Society's Perth branch, wrote: 'My husband, Lt. Col. T. Harris Hunter, 51st Division, R.A.S.C., who is a prisoner of war in Germany, started a Country Dance class there some time ago. Having forgotten some of the dances he asked me to send out a book. I have sent out "Twenty-Four Favourites" but don't know yet whether he has received it or not. They all seem very keen on Country Dancing and he has invented a new dance which he has called the 51st Division. I am so glad they have found another interest.'

Later in the Society's records the dance is briefly referred to as the 'St Valéry Reel', but there followed a letter home from the camp asking for the dance to be called The Reel of the 51st Division since the name St Valéry held so many sad memories.

The Reel of the 51st Division was destined to make a little more history for the Society which had always declared that its purpose was to collect, revive and publish old dances and not to countenance newly composed ones. The first exception to that rule was made for The Reel of the 51st Division which was passed round the branches of the Society very quickly by word of mouth and gained tremendous popularity in spite of not being an 'official' Society dance. Queen Elizabeth, now Queen Mother, also had a hand in the dance's adoption by the Society, when she asked for its inclusion in a Society book, as in her opinion it was such a lovely dance as well as being an historic one.

This was an excellent dance to prove the exception, since the figures were all absolutely conventional, the music, The Drunken Piper, perfectly in keeping with the dance, and the whole in the true spirit of the old dances.

Having made this exception, however, the Society was extremely careful not to encourage the creation of new dances by members and turned down smartly a suggestion that members be allowed to submit to the Society for criticism dances they had composed.

Branches of the Society which danced too many 'made-up' modern dances were soon reprimanded from Headquarters on the grounds that the purpose of country dancing was sociability and to dance the dances of their own creation, which others would not know, was to go against that precept. This did rather ignore the sound tradition of the 18th- and early 19th-century Golden Age when a Master of Ceremonies could make up dances on the spot by simply calling out figure after figure to a chosen tune.

The Society's disapproval was well intentioned. There was, it realized, enough work and pleasure to be found in the old dances, and the new continued to be accepted only very slowly after careful and prolonged consideration. However, today, the habit of creating new dances is rife – particularly among overseas members who are capable of presenting entire programmes of their own compositions.

And not only are new dances being created but new figures

have been introduced. The best of these – the tournet, the rondel and the knot – have been accepted by the Society, and are now regularly included in newly created dances, and they will prove useful to future historians when they come to the dating of dances. Just as a dance containing a poussette cannot have been in existence before 1790 or so, one containing the tournet, the rondel or the knot belongs to the post Second World War era.

After 1945, the Society quickly resumed its former activities – branch classes and dances, the summer school at St Andrews, the publication of dances. Now it encountered a problem, albeit a delightful one – almost too many people wanted to country dance. The wartime activities of the Society had been a propaganda machine par excellence and interest in the old dances, rather than fading away as it had after the First World War, blossomed as never before.

Now people country danced everywhere – in village halls and in the back rooms of pubs, in Scout huts and church halls, in the open air, in private houses. Public dance halls in the cities held 'Country Dance' nights which were usually crowded out, and on the dance programmes at public dances and private balls, foxtrots, modern waltzes and sambas and quicksteps were lavishly intermixed with Eightsome Reels, The Dashing White Sergeant, The Gay Gordons, Strip the Willow, The Reel of the 51st Division, The Duke of Perth.

In 1951 the Society's post-war success was crowned when it was granted the title 'Royal', partly in recognition of the tremendous work it had achieved in a comparatively brief space of time, and partly as an acknowledgement of the royal family's interest in its work.

On each royal visit to Scotland, the Society has presented a programme of dances for the royal family's entertainment at Holyrood Palace and Queen Elizabeth – now the Queen Mother, and a former pupil of Dancie Neill – has been an enthusiastic dancer all her life. This was an enthusiasm shared by both of her daughters and Princess Elizabeth became Patron of the Society in 1947.

On her accession to the throne in 1952, the Princess, as Queen Elizabeth II, let it be known that she wished to continue as Patron and thus she remains, visiting the Society's Edinburgh headquarters, attending important functions, such as the Society's Golden Jubilee Ball in Edinburgh in 1973, and taking a close personal interest in all the Royal Scottish Country Dance Society's activities.

Without doubt, in the post-war years, there was a second Golden Age of country dancing, and not only in Scotland. Just as in the time of the first Golden Age Scottish country dances and reels had become the rage of Europe, now they travelled abroad again.

During the early war years, the Society's first American branch was set up in New York, and branches soon began to spring up all over the United States and throughout Canada. An urgent need grew for Society-trained teachers to instruct new members and it became impractical for everyone who wished to gain a teaching certificate to come to centres in Britain for examination. Miss Milligan and her co-examiners were already conducting regular examinations at centres throughout Britain – so why not in other parts of the world?

Thus, hardly a year passes without official examinations being conducted at various centres abroad. Miss Milligan was still globe-trotting and spreading the word long past her ninetieth birthday.

There are branches of the Society established in most major centres in North America, in Africa, Canada, Australia and New Zealand. The Society's list of Branches and Affiliated Groups reads like a world gazetteer – from Alaska through Japan to Zambia. And in Japan in recent years Scottish country dancing has entered yet another Golden Age.

In Europe there are enthusiastic groups in every country in the West. In Paris, *Le Chardon d'Ecosse* country dancing club regularly assembles upwards of a hundred dancers. People in non-Commonwealth countries usually come to Scottish country dancing via an interest in folk dancing. They are, at first, intrigued and then, apparently, captivated by a style of native dancing which is ballroom dancing and which is above all happy, lively and sociable.

The second Golden Age of country dancing in Scotland lasted well into the 1960s. During that time Scottish country dance band leaders such as Jimmy Shand, Adam Rennie, Jim Cameron, Tim Wright and Ian Powrie became household names both at home and abroad. The remarkable revival of interest in the 1970s in the traditional fiddle music of Scotland had its roots in the years when folk would flock from miles around to dance to the music of a good, popular band.

Television, too, had its effect on the popularity of dancing. The BBC television service first began in Scotland in 1952 and among its earliest popular programmes was The Kilt is My Delight, a series made up of country dances. Later came The White Heather Club which initially included country dancing and Highland and step dancing.

These Highland and step dances, too, had passed into a new stage in their development. In response to requests from all over Scotland for standardization in the steps and figures of the old solo dances similar to that which the Scottish Country Dance Society had achieved for country dancing, the Scottish Official Board of Highland Dancing was set up in 1950. The Country Dance Society is represented on the SOBHD and Mrs Isobel Cramb of Aberdeen, a prominent member of the Royal Scottish Country Dance Society and a scholarly dance researcher, re-introduced into the Highland Dance Board's official repertoire several of the graceful step dances for women, in particular the dances so beloved of the 18th- and 19th-century dancing masters.

But, despite the Official Board's and the Country Dance Society's work and the painstaking authentication undertaken by Mrs Cramb, television dancing since the early 1960s has gone 'its ain gait' in Scotland. What is now presented as Scottish dancing on light entertainment programmes, is often a weird combination of simple ballet steps and a few flings and shuffles in shoddy imitation of the dancing-master tradition, with little regard for the vast repertoire of real dances that could well be called on to serve the purpose of entertainment. For those who love the old dances, it is a joy to see a dancer of the calibre of Brian Seivwright of Aberdeen, for example, dancing the genuine High dances – but sadly he rarely performs them on the small screen.

One remembers with nostalgia when TV screens were graced, and audiences enthralled, by the dancing of the matchless step/character/Highland/country dancer, Bobby Watson, who is also the last of the travelling dancies and a superb piper to boot.

The mass audiences who would rearrange their social lives in order not to miss these early dance programmes were a measure of the popularity of the art.

Then in the late years of the fifties and the early sixties a distinct gulf opened between the interests and activities of older and younger generations. After sixty years of popularity, the old American dances, the quickstep, the foxtrot, and so on, were suddenly engulfed in a flood of rock and roll and the Twist. The whole social dancing scene was transformed. While older people clung for a time to the old dances – and to each other! – the younger generation rocked and twisted to rhythmic music, not in sociable groups, not even in couples, but in gyrating solos which were an open rejection of every previous social dance form. Country dancing in the ballroom was simply not for the young – it was sometimes taught in school, but, in keeping with the rebellious spirit of the time, it was rejected outside and after school. Scottish country dancing was once again in dire danger of being eclipsed, perhaps, this time, for ever.

Instead it has become almost an art form in urban Scotland,

practised in cities and towns by large groups of enthusiasts. In the countryside, and among the military, country dances have remained part of social dance programmes, and, in rural areas in particular, the younger generation knows enough about the form of the dances to step out some of the old favourites.

Accepting, then, that country dancing is no longer the principal – if still the only truly native – ballroom dancing of Scotland, it might seem prudent to end this story here with a suitable chord and a curtsey.

But that would be to ignore the continuing and ever-growing influence and activities of the Royal Scottish Country Dance Society in Scotland and abroad.

Each summer, as in the earliest days, hundreds of country dancers of many nationalities converge on St Andrews to spend a fortnight studying the Society's most recent book of dances, receiving tuition in country-dance and solo steps, learning something about the music and its importance to the dances. Dancers are schooled by a staff which was headed, until her death in 1978, by the redoubtable Miss Milligan – Dr Milligan when, in 1977, Aberdeen University bestowed upon her an honorary LL.D.

The summer school proved so popular that it now lasts for four weeks divided into two sessions and could, so over-subscribed is it, last for as many months.

Those attending the St Andrews' school are classified according to their own assessment into beginners', intermediate and advanced classes, and appropriate instruction is given at various venues throughout the town.

The advanced class enjoyed for years the benefit of daily instruction from Jean Milligan in lessons the participants would never forget. Each morning she took command of her class and sweetly dragooned them through the intricacies and nuances of the dances, often taking these proficient dancers back to the fundamental steps.

To watch Jean Milligan conduct one of these classes was to be aware of tremendous strength of character, enormous good humour, total dedication to the art of country dancing, and the spark of genius which had melded all of these into a small, stout, human powerhouse.

Her technique for teaching a new dance even to the most experienced of pupils was to have them walk it through to establish the basic figures, then to dance it figure by figure, giving tremendous attention to detail. Thereafter she polished and inspired.

'Dancing is a thing of the soul – the communion between the ear and the feet.

'Dance *with* your music – don't perform. So many perform when all they must do is dance.

'Character is everything! Dancing is the physical expression of character.

'Good manners in life, as in dancing, is the outward sign of a kind and thoughtful heart!

'I want you to think to yourselves, "I will do this exquisitely and elegantly, for Miss Milligan!" '

She was the modern embodiment of the finest of the old dancing masters, with a touch of Assembly Directress. She was also the possessor of a remarkable sense of the right music for the dance. A dance tune which did not match exactly the changes in figures, nor accentuate the climax of the dance, did not last exactly the right number of bars nor relate in key and mode to the mood of the dance, was anathema to her, and a considerable debt is owed to Miss Milligan for her revival of good tunes along with dances.

That tens of thousands of dancers now have dances to dance – more or less elegantly! – and that country dancing still has a place in Scotland's social life, is due almost entirely to the life's work of Jean Milligan and to the Royal Scottish Country Dance Society.

The dancies have almost entirely vanished from the scene. Highland dance teachers now rarely, if ever, teach social dances.

Yet the traditional love of dancing persists in Scotland and already there are signs that along with the great revival of interest in native fiddle music there is a growing general interest in the dances these tunes accompanied.

The Scots have always danced and they created for themselves a very special dance form which is a mixture of the formal, the traditional, the balletic, a simple love of movement and the work of the dancing masters and of the Royal Scottish Country Dance Society. But, just as one must guess at the very beginnings of a nation's dancing, one cannot forecast a continuing story.

Suffice it to say that so long as there's a good rousing tune or two, good company, and an excuse to dance, there will always be Scots handy with their feet.

SOME SOURCES AND FURTHER READING

Arbeau, Thoinot *Orchésographie* Langres 1588

Bremner, Robert *Collections of Scots Reels or Country Dances* Edinburgh and London 1751 onwards

Cockburn, Henry *Memorials of His Time* A. & C. Black, Edinburgh 1856; Mercat Press, Edinburgh 1971

Cockburn, Henry *Circuit Journeys* A. & C. Black, Edinburgh 1889

Compan's *Dictionnaire de Danse* Paris 1787

Coplande, Robert *The manner of dauncynge base daunces* London 1521

Cramb, Isobel *Francis Peacock 1723–1807* Aberdeen University Review Spring 1970

Emmerson, George S. *A Social History of Scottish Dance – Ane Celestial Recreatioun* McGill-Queen's University Press, Montreal and London 1971

Emmerson, George S. *Rantin' Pipe and Tremblin' String: A History of Scottish Dance Music* J. M. Dent, London 1971

Flett, J. F. and T. M. *Traditional Dancing in Scotland* Routledge and Kegan Paul, London

Grant, Elizabeth, Ed. Lady Strachey *Memoirs of a Highland Lady 1797–1827* J. Murray, London 1898, Ed. Anthony Davidson, J. Murray 1950

Guilcher, Jean-Michel *La Contredanse* Mouton, Paris 1969

Landrin, Pierre *Potpourris de Contredanses* Paris c. 1770 onwards

Mackie, J. D. *The History of Scotland* Penguin, London 1970

Milligan, Jean C. *Introducing Scottish Country Dancing* Collins, London 1968

Peacock, Francis *Sketches Relative to the History, Theory, but more especially to the Practice of Dancing* Aberdeen 1805

Smout, T. C. *A Social History of Scotland 1560–1830* Collins, London 1969; Fontana 1972

INDEX